A Primer on Microeconomics

A Primer on Microeconomics

Thomas Beveridge

A Primer on Microeconomics

First published in 2013 by
Business Expert Press, LLC
222 East 46th Street, New York, NY 10017
www.businessexpertpress.com

ISBN-13: 978-1-60649-421-9 (paperback)

ISBN-13: 978-1-60649-422-6 (e-book)

DOI 10.4128/9781606494226

Business Expert Press Economics collection

Collection ISSN: 2163-761X (print)
Collection ISSN: 2163-7628 (electronic)

Cover design by Jonathan Pennell
Interior design by Exeter Premedia Services Private Ltd.,
Chennai, India

First edition: 2013

10 9 8 7 6 5 4 3 2 1

Printed in the United States of America.

Abstract

Economics, far from being the "dismal science," offers us valuable lessons that can be applied to our everyday experiences. At its heart, economics is the science of choice and a study of economic principles allows us to achieve a more informed understanding of how we make our choices; regardless of whether these choices occur in our everyday life or in our work environment.

The present text represents a common sense approach to basic microeconomics. It is directed toward all students, but particularly those within business school settings including students beginning an advanced business degree course of study. It will deliver clear statements of essential economic principles, supported by easy to understand examples, and uncluttered by extraneous material; the goal being to provide a concise readable primer that covers the substance of microeconomic theory.

The text will look at the efficient operation of competitive markets and what may cause those markets to fail; the benefits from trade; profit maximization; the consequences of choice; and the implications of imperfect competition.

Keywords

comparative advantage, opportunity cost, demand and supply, equilibrium, elasticity, marginal benefit, consumer surplus, producer surplus, economic efficiency, profit maximization, perfect competition, market failures, monopoly, imperfect competition

Contents

Preface

This *Primer on Microeconomics* has been long in the writing. It has been shaped by after-class discussions with students over many years while we tried to break down economics into understandable concepts and examples. A former student, Dr. Jeff Edwards, now Chairman of the Economic Department at North Carolina A&T State University, requested that I write an introductory text, and advised "Make it like your lectures."

No book, at least no book that I'm capable of writing, can capture the immediacy and intimacy of a classroom environment but, equally, no classroom environment permits the opportunity to dwell on detail quite as effectively as the pages of a book. As with everything in economics, there are trade offs.

I've devised this *Primer* to help you to master the concepts in what may to be your first, and perhaps only, economics course. I've given you given opportunities to apply these concepts in real-world situations. Most economists stress the need for competence in three major areas—the application of economic concepts to real-world situations, the interpretation of graphs, and the analysis of numerical problems. This *Primer* allows you to develop these important skills. In addition, you may visit my website www.tbeveridge.com where additional learning support is available to you in the form of a chapter-by-chapter study guide, with exercises, applications and examples, and further learning experiences and tips. Feel free to contact me with questions and requests, and I'll be happy to respond as time permits.

Throughout the text, I've attempted to maintain the sense of a dialogue—there are frequent "Think it through" pauses, during which you can review and check your grasp of the topic under discussion.

I hope that this book will ignite in you a passion for economics that will blaze for a lifetime. Economics surrounds us—it fills the airwaves, our daily lives, our hopes and dreams. Learning how to apply economic concepts to our world creates a better and more durable understanding and a reasonable goal for a noneconomics major is to have sufficient insight to evaluate the economic content of articles in *The Wall Street Journal* or *The Economist* or the views expressed by commentators on CNN or Fox.

This *Primer* has been written with the hope that, long after you have turned the final page, you will retain a deeper understanding of economic issues and the tools to analyze the exciting and challenging concerns that we all must address in our contemporary world.

Best wishes to you in your study of economics. You will find it a rewarding and worthwhile experience, and I trust that this *Primer* will stimulate you in your endeavors.

Acknowledgments

Through the years, many students have asked me questions and, by doing so, have given me deeper insights into the difficulties that arise when Economics is first approached. I am grateful to all of them. Much of the material included in this book springs from such "after class" discussions.

The efforts of reviewers Phil Romero and Jeff Edwards have added greatly to the quality of the final product. A former student, Jonas Feit, now thriving at North Carolina State University, critiqued early drafts. Cindy Durand of Business Expert Press deserves credit for keeping things moving smoothly. Denver Harris has been stalwart and reliable in converting a misshapen, poorly-written manuscript into an orderly text. Needless to say, any remaining *lapsi calami* are my responsibility.

This *Primer* is dedicated, with love, to the memory of my parents, Pam (my long-suffering wife), Andrew (whose surprises are no longer shocks but delights), and to the dogs and cats, and especially to Cody, for whom all lunches are free.

Thomas Beveridge
Hillsborough, North Carolina

CHAPTER 1

Scarcity and Choice

By the end of this chapter you will be able to:

1. Identify the three fundamental economic questions.
2. Explain why a production possibility frontier has a negative slope and why that slope depicts the concept of opportunity cost.
3. Interpret what is depicted by a production possibility frontier.
4. Explain why increasing opportunity costs occur in the real world and how this relates to the production possibility frontier diagram.
5. Use the production possibility frontier to identify how economic growth might occur.
6. Distinguish between productive efficiency and allocative efficiency.
7. Distinguish between absolute advantage and comparative advantage.
8. Use comparative advantage to explain the theory that individuals or countries can gain from specialization and exchange.

Economics: The Scientific Study of Rational Choice

Imagine you're in a restaurant and the server has just handed you the menu. You are preparing to make a choice. You have entered the realm of economics. At its most fundamental, economics is about choice. We may define economics as the scientific study of rational choice. Although that assumption of rationality has recently come under some attack, it remains a good working assumption. We make choices as we strive to achieve the best outcomes possible in our own self-interest. Individually and as a society, we must make choices because, although we have unlimited wants, we have limited (scarce) resources to meet those wants.

Scarcity

In economics, an item is considered "scarce" if, when its price is zero, then there is not enough of the item available to satisfy our requirements. If a good has a positive price tag then it's scarce. Can you think of any "free" (nonscarce) goods? Is clean air a free good or is it scarce?

Resources

Economists define four types of scarce resource.

Natural resources include any usable naturally occurring resources. Farmland, a navigable river, or lobsters off the coast of Maine are examples of natural resources.

Capital resources are reusable tools—goods that are produced to make other goods. Private capital includes a carpenter's chisel, a sales rep's car, or a warehouse whereas social capital includes the nation's roads, bridges, and docks.

Human resources ("labor") include all of the mental and physical attributes of the labor force, such as the shooting ability of LeBron James, the physical stamina of a fruit picker, or the specialized skills and knowledge of a brain surgeon. As an aside, if a worker trains and acquires new skills, this acquisition is termed "human capital." Education of any kind that increases our abilities is an investment in human capital.

Finally, **enterprise** ("entrepreneurial ability") is the risk-taking talent needed to recognize unfulfilled market opportunities and organize production to meet those needs.

The rewards for the use of these four classes of resources are rent, interest, wages and salaries, and profit, respectively. The farmer who lets a neighbor use his tractor during harvest would receive an interest payment but if he lets him use some unneeded acreage, then the payment is rent. The farm laborer receives a wage or salary. The farmer (the owner of an enterprise) hopes to earn a profit for himself.

Comment: In economics, unlike in accounting, profit (more properly, a "normal" profit, which is a reasonable rate of return for the entrepreneur) is treated the same as wages and salaries, rent, and interest. Just as those other payments represent costs of doing business, so does profit. We will return to this point later in the chapter.

Caution #1: Although money can be used to buy or hire productive resources, it in itself is not a productive resource. A trunk filled with dollars washed up on Robinson Crusoe's island would do him no good at all. It has no productive value.

Caution #2: Terms used in economics may not mean the same as in regular speech. "Rent" is a good example. Apartment-dwellers pay "rent" to their "landlord," but most of that payment is not for the use of a natural resource (the space the apartment occupies); it's for the structure itself, and for the wiring and plumbing and other man-made (capital) features being used. "Investment" (the addition to the stock of capital) is another term with a very specific meaning in economics.

THINK IT THROUGH: Every productive activity involves some combination of those four categories of scarce resource. Think of your own work environment and identify examples of each of the four types of resource. It is almost impossible to specify a productive activity that does not involve human resources, natural resources, capital, and enterprise. Try it!

The Economic Challenge and Three Fundamental Questions

The economic challenge, then, is to find the way to best satisfy our unlimited wants with our limited resources. The three fundamental questions that must be answered by any economy are "What to Produce?", "How to Produce?", and "How Do We Distribute Production?" Every economy must transform its scarce natural, capital, and human resources into usable production through the application of enterprise. In a complex society, the opportunity to cooperate and specialize offers great scope for increased production—but decisions must be made regarding the extent of cooperation, who specializes in what, and how goods are distributed. Even Robinson Crusoe and Friday on their island must come up with answers to these questions. Wants are limitless, but resources are scarce. We are compelled to make choices.

As a restaurant owner, because you cannot offer everything, you must decide *which* items will be on your menu (what to produce). You must also determine *how* your service will be produced (*cordon-bleu* chef or a microwave; self-service or servers; and so on). Finally, you must come up with a method of allocating your production among your potential customers (first-come first-serve or reservations; all you can eat or *à la carte*).

The trick is to choose the most effective technique in order to produce "the right stuff." In our economy, although there is a role for the public provision of certain goods and services such as national defense or our justice system, we mainly use private markets to answer the three fundamental questions. We produce items that can earn a profit as cheaply as possible (in order to make the most profit) and provide them to those who are able to pay the price.

THINK IT THROUGH: When the *Titanic* sank in 1912, there were limited spaces available in the lifeboats. The collision with the iceberg posed an immediate "distribution" question—who gets the lifeboat seats? The traditional solution of "Women and children first!" was largely adhered to (most babies and children and a high proportion of women survived) although upper-class males seem to have been given priority over steerage passengers. If "Women and children first" were not used to allocate lifeboat seats, what other methods would have been effective in such a crisis situation?

THINK IT THROUGH: Can you think of other "rules" that our society has developed to apportion our limited goods and services?

Opportunity Cost

Choice is at the heart of economics. Any time we make a choice, there is a cost. Economists use the term "opportunity cost." Opportunity cost is the value of the next most preferred alternative given up when you make a choice. This idea of opportunity cost is both simple and profound—there's no such thing as a free lunch, as the saying goes. In the restaurant, if you order shrimp lo mein, then you give up the opportunity to have other items on the menu. If the shrimp had not been available, the value you place on the item you would have chosen instead is the opportunity cost of the shrimp.

Remember: Whenever you make a choice, you are choosing to accept one option (A) but you are also choosing to give up all the other options (B, C, and so on). Opportunity cost is the value you place of the second-best option. The value of the option selected should exceed its opportunity cost otherwise you've not made a rational choice. Note that our opportunity cost definition doesn't refer explicitly to a financial cost. Even if a friend is paying the tab, it's still not a free lunch for you because you are making choices. Choosing the New York strip means that you can't choose your next-favorite option.

Production Possibility Frontier

The production possibility frontier (PPF) diagram can be used to depict choice and opportunity cost. A PPF diagram shows precisely what its name suggests—the frontier (or boundary) between what is possible to produce and what is not possible to produce, given the most effective use of our resources and our technology. We know already what our resources consist of (human resources, natural resources, capital, and enterprise), but what is "technology"? **Technology** is our method of combining our resources. If we develop a method of combining our resources that increases output, then this is a technological advance. A better crop rotation system in farming would be an example. Can you think of others?

In a world where two goods are produced (say, guns and butter) and where all resources are fully employed, if we allocate more of our resources to produce guns then fewer resources are available to produce butter and less butter will be produced—there is a trade-off. The opportunity cost of choosing to produce more guns is the butter we can no longer produce.

Following from this conclusion, it is clear that the PPF must have a negative slope. More guns mean less butter.

Suppose we have a small firm that produces two goods—wooden chairs and tables. We have workers and other resources. Each hour, using the best available production methods (technology), there can be only a finite quantity of chairs we can produce. Let's say six chairs. We can plot this option (6 chairs, 0 tables) on the vertical axis of Figure 1-1 at point A. Similarly, there are only so many tables we can produce—perhaps three tables. We can plot this option (0 chairs, 3 tables) on the horizontal axis at point D. If we're currently producing six chairs then, if we increase the production of tables, we will have to pull resources away from chair production. Chair production will decrease as table production increases— there is a negative relationship between them.

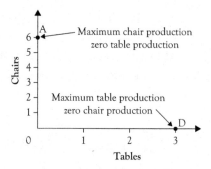

Figure 1-1. Constructing a production possibility frontier.

So far, we have the two endpoints of the PPF and we know that it must have a negative slope. The frontier's slope represents the rate at which one good is given up as more of the other good is produced. This rate, known formally as the *marginal rate of transformation*, describes opportunity cost. For example, if we produce one more table, the opportunity cost is the number of chairs we will no longer be able to produce.

The Law of Increasing Cost

This rate of trade-off is unlikely to remain constant as we increase the production of chairs because not all resources are equally well suited to different activities. Think back to high school and the choosing of teams for basketball. Just as some players were better than others and would be chosen first, some resources will be more productive in chair production than others and will be preferred.

Suppose we have three workers—Abe, Bill, and Calvin—whose hourly outputs are listed as follows.

Production Alternatives			Opportunity Cost of One	
Tables		Chairs	Table	Chair
Abe	1	or	1	1 chair	1 table
Bill	1	or	2	2 chairs	1/2 table
Calvin	1	or	3	3 chairs	1/3 table

Who would you choose first to produce tables? And who would be your next choice? You should choose Abe first to produce tables, then Bill, and, finally, Calvin because Abe can produce tables at the lowest (opportunity) cost. With Abe, the table he produces "costs" one chair but, if Calvin produces a table, then we must give up the three chairs he could otherwise have produced. Looked at differently, we should keep Calvin producing chairs as long as possible because he is so good at chair production.

Note that, as we expand production of tables, the opportunity cost of tables increases. The first table (Abe's) costs one chair, Bill's costs two chairs, and Calvin's costs three chairs. The production alternatives are listed as follows.

Production Alternatives	Tables	Chairs
A	0	6
B	1	5
C	2	3
D	3	0

We can plot these alternatives. Graphically, as shown in Figure 1-2, the PPF bends outwards. The slope of the PPF depicts the increasing opportunity cost we have discussed.

THINK IT THROUGH: Verify that, if the workers are all producing tables, and we switch them over to producing chairs, we should switch Calvin first, then Bill, and finally Abe. Opportunity cost again increases as we expand the production of chairs.

Comment on Reciprocals: Note that, for Calvin, the opportunity cost of producing one table is three chairs and the opportunity cost of one

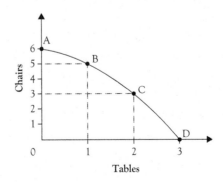

Figure 1-2. Production possibility frontier.

chair is a third of a table. The opportunity costs are reciprocals of each other. If Calvin is the least costly at producing chairs then he necessarily must be the most costly at producing tables. This is a general result and we'll use it later in this chapter when we look at comparative advantage.

Marginal Cost: Let's press this example a little further. Economists, as we shall see later, are deeply concerned with "marginal" analysis. "Marginal" is just a fancy term economists use, meaning "extra" or "additional." **Marginal cost** is the additional cost incurred when an extra unit of a good is produced. (Similarly, marginal benefit is the additional benefit that is received when an extra unit of a good is consumed.) Superficially, we think of "the additional cost incurred when an extra unit of a good is produced" in terms of dollars and cents but, more profoundly, it is the opportunity cost. Alone on his island, Robinson Crusoe has no money but, because he makes choices, he incurs costs. Choosing to produce more chairs results in increasing costs. The extra cost of the first table was one chair, but the second table cost two chairs, and the third table's cost was higher still. Typically, because of the law of increasing cost, we'd predict that the marginal cost would increase as more tables are produced.

THINK IT THROUGH: If the cost of producing additional tables increases, what must happen to the price of tables in order to encourage the producer to boost output?

Constant Costs

An outward-bending PPF depicts increasing cost. However, if the PPF is a straight downward-sloping line, then the opportunity cost is constant. This would happen if resources were identical in abilities. If the PPF were to bend inward, then this would tell us that opportunity cost is decreasing—in real-world terms, improbable.

Any PPF diagram has three regions—the frontier itself, inside the frontier, and beyond the frontier. Consider Figure 1-3. Any point on the frontier (such as point K) represents a point of maximum production; any point inside the frontier (such as point L) indicates underproduction; and any point beyond the frontier (such as point M) is an option that is not attainable given our current resources and technology.

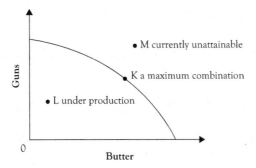

Figure 1-3. The components of a production possibility frontier.

Although increasing costs are typical in the real world, from now on we will assume that producers face constant opportunity costs, because this will allow us to draw the simpler straight-line PPFs.

Note: If we have constant costs, then marginal cost is constant, rather than increasing, as output increases.

Relaxing the Diagram's Assumptions

The PPF is drawn on the basis of a given set of resources and a given best way of combining them. If we get more or better resources, or an improved way of combining our given resources, then there will be a general increase in what it is possible to produce. In such a case, the PPF will shift outwards from PPF1 to PPF2, as shown in Figure 1-4. A decrease in the quantity or quality of resources will shift the whole curve inwards as what it is possible to produce is diminished.

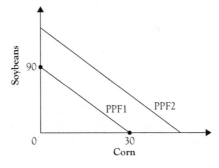

Figure 1-4. A general increase in the production possibility frontier.

A resource or technology change could be specific to only one good. In farming, for example, a strain of corn with a higher yield might be developed. In this case, although the maximum production of soybeans would be unaltered, the maximum production of corn would increase, causing the PPF to pivot from PPF1 to PPF2, as shown in Figure 1-5. Observe that the slope of the PPF has changed. Because the slope of the frontier depicts opportunity cost, then the opportunity cost of corn (and thus soybeans) must have changed.

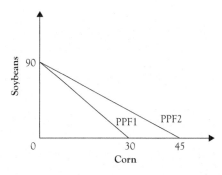

Figure 1-5. A good-specific increase in the production possibility frontier.

Consider the slope of PPF1 and its endpoints. If we choose to produce only corn then we can produce 30 units of corn, but we must give up the 90 units of soybeans that could have been produced. Each unit of corn "costs" three units of soybeans. Now consider the slope of PPF2. If we choose to produce only corn then we can produce 45 units of corn, but we must give up the 90 units of soybeans. Each unit of corn now "costs" only two units of soybeans. The opportunity cost of corn has decreased. Verify that the opportunity cost of a unit of soybeans has increased from one-third of a unit of corn to one-half of a unit of corn.

THINK IT THROUGH: What happened to Europe's PPF during the Black Death? What was the effect on American production of the introduction of the Internet in the 1990s? Finally, in 1945, the Manhattan Project developed the atomic bomb. In terms of "guns and butter," how did the Allies' PPF change? Show each of these cases with a PPF diagram.

Using the PPF Diagram

We have now developed an understanding of the general meaning of the PPF and the assumptions behind it. But how can it be used? The analysis can be used in several ways, for instance, when thinking about the consequences of choice, different concepts of efficiency, the distinction between microeconomics and macroeconomics, and the basis for trade.

The PPF illustrates choice. Along the frontier, where we have full employment of resources, if we choose to produce more guns, the consequence is that we must settle for less butter. The slope of the frontier shows the rate of trade-off and reminds us that "there's no such thing as a free lunch."

Comment: Note, though, that if we have unemployed resources, we may be able to produce more guns without giving up any butter. There need be no opportunity cost in this situation.

Efficiency: The PPF can also be used to distinguish between two differing concepts of efficiency. Consider Figure 1-6.

Any point on the frontier is a point of maximum **productive efficiency**. In this sense of producing at maximum capacity, points A, B, C, and D are all equally "efficient." Point E is inefficient because some of our scarce resources are being squandered—we could be producing at a higher level.

However, there's more to life than simply producing lots of stuff. Our economy ought to produce "the right stuff." Consider the figure once more. Are points A, B, C, and D equal in terms of satisfying our wants?

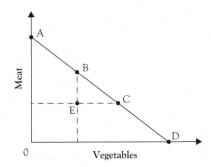

Figure 1-6. Productive efficiency and allocative efficiency.

Clearly not! If we are a society of vegans then point A (all meat, no vegetables) is a less desirable option than point D. Not all points on the frontier are equivalent in terms of **allocative efficiency** (producing the mixture of goods that society prefers the most). In fact, point A is less desirable than point E (where we get at less some vegetables).

The two "efficiency" concepts are distinct. In terms of productive efficiency, any point on the PPF is superior to any point inside the frontier. However, in terms of allocative efficiency, a given point inside the frontier may be preferred to some points on the frontier. (As a general rule though, there must be at least one point on the frontier that is superior to any point inside. Point C, for example, is preferred to point E because society gets more vegetables without losing any meat.)

Comment: Intuitively, productive efficiency may be thought of as "activity" while allocative efficiency may be thought of as "achievement."

Microeconomics Versus Macroeconomics: Microeconomics generally starts from the assumption that society is already at a point on its PPF and can be thought of as examining how we might move the production mix to a point of greater allocative efficiency along the line. Macroeconomics, which considers the consequences of unemployment or lackluster growth, may be thought of as exploring how we might either move toward the frontier or, indeed, shift the frontier itself.

Comparative Advantage and the Basis for Trade

The PPF and opportunity cost can be used to examine the basis for specialization and trade. The roots of this analysis reach back to the early nineteenth century and the British economist, David Ricardo, who developed the Law of Comparative Advantage.

Briefly, assuming two participants (Jack and Jill), two goods (bread and wine), and constant costs (straight-line PPFs), if Jack and Jill's opportunity costs differ, then it must be the case that each individual must have a "*comparative advantage*" in the production of one of the two goods. The one exception to this would be if the opportunity costs were identical. We can make this analysis a little easier if we realize that the comparative advantage referred to is an opportunity cost advantage. If, relatively, Jack can produce wine at a lower opportunity cost than Jill, (that is, Jack has a comparative cost advantage in wine production), then Jill must be able to

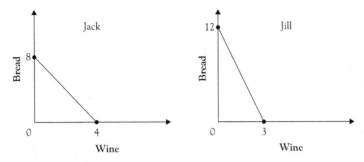

Figure 1-7. The graphical basis for trade.

produce bread at a lower opportunity cost than Jack (that is, a comparative cost advantage in bread production).

This may seem a curious conclusion. An obvious objection to raise would be "But what if Jack can produce both goods more cheaply than Jill?" Such a situation is impossible. Recall the tables and chairs example where we concluded that each worker's opportunity cost of producing a chair is the reciprocal of his opportunity cost of producing a table. Relatively, the greater the cost advantage a worker has in the production of one good, the greater the cost disadvantage he has in the production of the other good.

Consider Figure 1-7. Jack, specializing only in bread production, can bake eight loaves each day, while Jill, similarly devoted to bread production can bake twelve loaves each day. Jill can produce more loaves perhaps because of superior skill, better ingredients, or a more reliable oven. Fully devoted to wine production, Jack can produce four bottles each day, but Jill (less skilled perhaps, or with less good grapes) can produce only three. Recall that the slope of the PPF depicts opportunity cost so the straight lines indicate that the opportunity costs are constant for each individual. The differing slopes indicate that the opportunity costs between individuals are different.

The **Law of Comparative (Cost) Advantage** states that Jack and Jill will benefit from specialization and trade if their opportunity costs (and the slopes of the frontiers) differ.

We must determine who should produce what good by comparing opportunity costs. For Jack, the opportunity cost of producing eight loaves is the four bottles of wine he is no longer able to produce—one loaf costs half a bottle of wine. Using the reciprocal trick, one bottle of wine "costs" two loaves. For Jill, the opportunity cost of producing twelve loaves is the three bottles of wine she can no longer produce—one loaf costs a fourth of a bottle of wine. Using the reciprocal trick, one bottle of wine "costs" four loaves.

Jack can produce wine cheaper (he has a comparative advantage in wine) while Jill can produce bread cheaper (she has a comparative advantage in bread). As long as the slopes of the PPFs differ, then it must be true that one producer has a comparative advantage in one good and the other producer has the comparative advantage in the other good. Again, because of reciprocity, no individual can have a comparative advantage in both goods.

Caution: "But," you say, "this result is obvious. Jack is better at wine production because he can produce more wine than Jill, and Jill is better at bread production because she can produce more loaves than Jack!" This is false logic. You have fallen into the trap of absolute advantage. In absolute terms, while it is true that Jack is superior to Jill in wine production and Jill trumps Jack in bread production, this fact has no bearing on how the two parties should specialize.

The fallacy is easy to show. Suppose that Jack can produce more wine and more bread than Jill. Does this mean that Jack should produce everything and that Jill should produce nothing? Clearly not. In the real world, there are large countries with many resources and small countries with few, but the small countries can still gain from trade and can contribute to general prosperity despite an absolute disadvantage in all goods.

We can summarize the results thus far.

Opportunity cost of:	Jack	Jill	Comparative advantage
one loaf of bread	1/2 bottle	1/4 bottle	Jill
one bottle of wine	2 loaves	4 loaves	Jack

Jack and Jill decide to specialize according to comparative advantage and trade with each other. Is mutually beneficial trade possible? Let's assume that Jack and Jill barter their trade goods, wine and bread, respectively. If the "price" of a bottle of wine is two loaves then Jack will not gain from trade (as his cost of production of a bottle of wine is also two loaves) but Jill will gain from trade. (Can you verify this?) If the "price" of a bottle of wine rises to four loaves then Jack gains from trade but Jill will not gain because, if the price of wine is four loaves then the price of bread is a quarter of a bottle of wine, which equals Jill's cost of production—her cost and the price at which she is trading are equal.

Between these two prices for a bottle of wine (two loaves and four loaves) lies a range of prices that will benefit both traders. Consider the situation where one wine is traded for three loaves. Jack, producing wine at a cost of two loaves, will gain because the price exceeds his cost. Similarly, but less obviously, Jill, producing bread at a cost of a quarter of a bottle of wine per loaf, will also gain because the price of a loaf (one-third of a bottle of wine) is also higher than her cost. Both benefit.

There is no requirement that both benefit equally—it depends on relative negotiating abilities, for example. As long as the price lies between the limits where one party or the other does not gain (one wine sells for two loaves and one wine sells for four loaves) trade will be mutually beneficial.

Comment: The **terms of trade** is the technical term for the "price" or the barter rate of exchange such as when one bottle of wine trades for two loaves.

Caution: We have concluded that the Law of Comparative Advantage persuades us that trade can be beneficial. Before moving on, it's worth noting that the analysis depends on the assumption that each person (or economy) is fully employed. If that is not the case, then the basis for trade (being on the PPF and, from there, opportunity cost) evaporates. Our opportunity cost calculations are valid only along the frontier itself. A nation struggling through a recession might still find it to be in its own best interests to restrict imports.

Trade when Preferences Differ and Endowments Do Not

In the example with Jack and Jill producing bread and wine and jointly determining whether or not there is a basis for trade, we assumed that the two parties had identical preferences and differing endowments of resources. It is the difference in endowments—resources, if you will—that makes Jack's PPF differ from Jill's. However, this is not the only possible case—individuals do not always have identical preferences. Is there still a basis for mutually advantageous trade if, for example, preferences differ but endowments are identical?

Let us suppose that there is a refugee camp somewhere in Latin America and two of the inmates are Juan and Carlos. They have differing preferences—Juan is a lifelong smoker with a severe nicotine addiction whereas, although he does smoke on occasion, Carlos's passion is candy. Carlos is known in the camp as having a sweet tooth.

Every so often a Red Cross truck arrives at the refugee camp and delivers a parcel to each inmate—each parcel contains 10 cigarettes and 20 pieces of chocolate candy. At the start of the analysis, Juan and Carlos have differing preferences by the same initial endowment. Can beneficial trade occur?

We ask Juan to determine how much satisfaction he will derive from his parcel of 10 cigarettes and 20 pieces of candy—economists call satisfaction "*utility*"—and, after a little thought, Juan comes up with an answer. His answer (how much satisfaction or utility he will derive from the 10 cigarettes and 20 pieces of candy) depends on how much he likes cigarettes and how much he likes candy.

Thought Experiment: We now ask Juan to participate in a thought experiment. We ask him to tell us what will happen to his level of satisfaction if we were to give him two more cigarettes. His satisfaction will increase by some amount because he has the same amount of candy as before but more cigarettes. Finally, we say that we will remove some of his candy, piece by piece, causing his satisfaction to decline, and we ask him to tell us when so much candy has been removed that his satisfaction level has been restored to its original (10 cigarettes and 20 pieces of candy) level. He stops us when we have taken away 10 pieces of candy. We have established that the two "bundles" of goods—10 cigarettes and 20 pieces of candy (bundle A) and 12 cigarettes and 10 pieces of candy (bundle B)—are equivalent for Juan. The results are given in Table 1-1.

With Carlos, we repeat the process, but with a slight difference—first we ask him to decide how much satisfaction he derives from his Red Cross parcel of 10 cigarettes and 20 pieces of candy. We then ask what will happen to his level of satisfaction if we were to remove 2 of his 10 cigarettes. Clearly, his satisfaction will decrease by some amount—how much will depend on how much he likes cigarettes and candy. We tell him that we will compensate him for the loss of his cigarettes by

Table 1-1. *Thought Experiments for Juan and Carlos*

		Juan		Carlos	
	Bundle	Cigarettes	Candy	Cigarettes	Candy
A	Red Cross Parcel	10	20	10	20
B = A	Thought Experiment	12	10	8	22

"paying" him candy and we ask him to say when he has been paid enough candy to compensate him fully for his loss and to restore his original (10 cigarettes and 20 pieces of candy) level of satisfaction. He stops us when we have given him two extra pieces of candy.

Our thought experiment has established that Carlos is indifferent between bundle A (10 cigarettes and 20 pieces of candy) and bundle B (8 cigarettes and 22 pieces of candy). The results are given in Table 1-1.

To recap, currently Juan and Carlos each has Bundle A, the Red Cross parcel—the thought experiment was just that, a thought experiment.

Let us now introduce a trader—Pedro. Pedro approaches Juan and offers to give him 2 cigarettes in exchange for 9 pieces of candy, leaving Juan with 12 cigarettes for 11 pieces of candy. Juan should accept because this bundle (bundle C) is superior to bundle B (more candy) and bundle B is equivalent to him to bundle A. (Juan should haggle, but let us ignore that.) By trading, Juan improves his satisfaction.

Similarly, Pedro approaches Carlos and offers to give him 3 pieces of candy for 2 cigarettes, leaving Carlos with 8 cigarettes and 23 pieces of candy (bundle C). Like Juan, Carlos should accept the trade because bundle C is superior to bundle B (more candy) and bundle B is equivalent to him to bundle A; therefore, bundle C is superior to bundle A. See Table 1-2.

Pedro's payment from trading is the 6 pieces of candy he receives. (There were 40—Juan has 11, Carlos has 23, and Pedro has 6.) This is Pedro's payment for acting as a middleman. He is providing a distribution service. It is possible for Juan and Carlos to get together and trade cigarettes and candy, dividing all of the goods between themselves and excluding Pedro, but this may be inconvenient to them.

THINK IT THROUGH: If you wish to borrow money to buy a car, you could approach friends, relatives, work colleagues, and strangers, and ask each

Table 1-2. Trades with Pedro and Pancho

	Bundle	Juan		Carlos	
		Cigarettes	Candy	Cigarettes	Candy
A	Red Cross Parcel	10	20	10	20
B (= A)	Thought Experiment	12	10	8	22
C (> A)	Pedro	12	11	8	23
D (> C)	Pancho	12	12	8	24

of them to lend you a few dollars, haggle over the terms of the loans, and sign a number of loan contracts. This, though, is inconvenient and a waste of your time—it's far easier and more efficient to visit the loan officer at your bank. The bank, by collecting the unused funds of depositors and redirecting those funds to borrowers who need financial capital, is acting as an intermediary and charges a price for this service—the interest rate paid by the borrower. Likewise, Pedro is providing a service and deserves to be paid for his trouble.

THINK IT THROUGH: There is an opportunity cost involved in trading. Let us suppose that Pedro or any other trader values his next-best alternative, say, sitting under a shade tree relaxing with his friends, at two pieces of candy. If Pedro receives six pieces of candy in payment, then, in some sense, his profit is four pieces of candy. As we shall see, economists term this profit that is over-and-above opportunity cost the *economic profit*.

The next time the Red Cross parcels arrive at the camp, another entrepreneur—Pancho—appears on the scene. Pancho has observed the economic profit—four pieces of candy—that Pedro has been earning on his trades and wishes to get in on the action. He approaches Juan and, in order to encourage Juan to trade with him, offers him a better deal that Pedro's—2 cigarettes in exchange for 8 pieces of candy, leaving Juan with 12 cigarettes for 12 pieces of candy. This bundle of goods (bundle D) is superior to bundle C (Pedro's offer) and Juan will benefit by accepting it.

Pancho then approaches Carlos and offers to give him 4 pieces of candy for return for 2 cigarettes, leaving Carlos with 8 cigarettes and 24 pieces of candy (bundle D). Bundle D is superior to bundle C (Pedro's offer) and Carlos will gain by accepting it. Pancho's payment from trading is the 4 pieces of candy he receives. (Initially, there were 40—Juan has

12, Carlos has 24, and Pancho has 4.) If Pancho values his next-best alternative to negotiating in the hot sun, sitting under a shade tree, at two pieces of candy, then his economic profit is two pieces of candy.

THINK IT THROUGH: Note that all the trading parties have gained. Pedro did not gain, but he was not a participant in this round of trading.

When Pedro was the only trader, the payment he received was six pieces of candy. With Pancho in competition, the payment was cut to four pieces of candy, as each trader tried to attract customers to him. If an additional trader (Pablo) were now to enter the market and compete for customers with Pedro and Pancho, then we can see that the traders' payment would be driven even lower.

How low will the payment go? Not to zero—for no one would be willing to accept the risk and inconvenience of trading for no payment at all. The answer is determined by opportunity cost. A trader will participate if the reward he receives is "worth it," that is, if it covers his opportunity cost. If the opportunity cost of trading is the value placed on socializing with friends under a shade tree and if that value is two pieces of candy, then the lowest payment that will encourage traders to enter the market is two pieces of candy. This payment, equal to and determined by opportunity cost, is a reasonable payment for their time and trouble, and economists call it a *normal profit*. In economics, unlike in accounting, normal profit (a reasonable rate of return for the entrepreneur) is treated the same as wages and salaries, rent, and interest. Just as those other payments represent costs of doing business, so does normal profit. Any payment received above the amount that covers opportunity cost is considered economic profit.

THINK IT THROUGH: This is an important point that we will revisit in Chapter 5 and, unfortunately, quite subtle and elusive. Accountants and, with them, the general public, are used to adding up business costs, subtracting the total from revenues and designating the difference "profit." According to this view, profit, then, is what remains *after* costs have been subtracted. Economists, on the other hand, consider some portion of profit—normal profit—to be part of the cost of doing business. In economics, "profit" has two components—normal profit (based on opportunity cost) and economic profit.

Lessons: We can learn some important lessons from this example.

Lesson 1: If participants have the same endowments but different preferences, then trade can be mutually beneficial. This is true whether Juan and Carlos prefer to trade with each other or prefer to use intermediaries.

Lesson 2: It is self-interest and the desire to earn a profit that prompts Pedro and the other entrepreneurs to provide goods or, as in this case, services. Entrepreneurs, seeing profit opportunities, will enter the market.

Lesson 3: Competition among traders can be expected to drive down profit margins until only a normal profit is earned. At that point, there is no incentive for additional entrepreneurs to enter the market and the market will stabilize. It is opportunity cost that determines the level of normal profit.

Lesson 4 (following from Lesson 3): Competition is beneficial for customers such as Juan and Carlos. Because competition drives down the profit received by entrepreneurs, as competition increases and profit margins decline, Juan and Carlos retain more of their candy and, therefore, gain more.

Lesson 5: There is an incentive for entrepreneurs to collude to reduce competition. Although competition benefits customers, it hurts entrepreneurs because it reduces their profits—ultimately to the point at which only a normal profit is being earned. Entrepreneurs have an incentive to collude to fix prices or to impose barriers to entry in order to reduce competition and keep profits high.

Lesson 6 (following from Lesson 5): Such collusive or restrictive action hurts consumers and reduces market efficiency.

Review: In this chapter we have discovered that "there is no such thing as a free lunch," in the sense that, any time a choice is made an alternative is chosen, but another alternative is given up. The value placed on the next-best alternative that is given up when a choice is made is its *opportunity cost*—perhaps the single most important idea in economics. When we look at "cost" in future chapters, keep in mind that, at its most profound level, it is opportunity cost that is involved.

CHAPTER 2

Demand and Supply

By the end of this chapter you will be able to:

1. State and explain the law of demand and the law of supply.
2. Draw and interpret demand and supply graphs.
3. Distinguish between a shift of a demand or supply curve and a movement along a curve, and show these cases correctly on a graph.
4. Determine equilibrium price and quantity and explain how the market adjusts when demand or supply changes.
5. Define shortage and surplus and predict their effects on the market price.
6. Specify the determinants of demand and supply and indicate how each must change for demand and supply to increase or decrease.
7. Distinguish between two goods that are substitutes and two goods that are complements.
8. Distinguish between normal and inferior goods.

George Bernard Shaw once jokingly remarked that if you taught a parrot to squawk the phrase "demand and supply" then you had trained an economist. Certainly it's true that demand and supply analysis is the lingua franca of economics.

Chapter Preview: Undoubtedly, you already use demand and supply analysis in your daily life. Just as we don't need to have learned applied physics or geometry (force, angles) in order to play pool, we don't need a course in economics to tell us that, if a war breaks out in the Middle East, then we should expect a price hike in a gallon of gasoline or that, if worker benefits increase in this country, then illegal immigration and outsourcing are likely to increase.

Examples of Using Demand and Supply Analysis Informally

Suppose there is a late freeze in Florida that destroys much of the orange crop. What will happen to the price of orange juice? It will increase (because the supply of a key ingredient has been reduced). What if news reveals that apples have been sprayed with an insecticide that causes cancer? We'll buy fewer apples and the price will fall (because demand has decreased). If the government imposes a carbon tax on gasoline-fueled cars, predict what will happen to the demand for electric cars. They'll become more popular! And, as they become more popular, will we expect more (or fewer) electric cars to be marketed? More! If Burger King raises the prices of its menu items, will you start going to McDonald's more or less frequently (assuming you go at all!)?

So we are already quite familiar with thinking about markets and, in practice, using demand and supply analysis. All of these situations can be investigated using demand and supply analysis.

In this chapter, we develop a model of how individuals interact within markets. A market is a location, physical or otherwise, where buyers and sellers interact.

Demand

We can define **demand** as the willingness and ability to purchase a quantity of a good or service at a range of prices during some time period. To be part of the demand for a good we must be both willing and able to buy. Many of us would be willing to buy a sleek Ferrari sports car but few of us are able to: only the few who are able and willing are demanders at the high price that Ferrari sets. Note that our definition of demand carries the notion that there is a time frame. It makes no sense to talk about "the demand for bananas," but it does make sense to refer to "the demand for bananas per week," "the demand for gasoline per month," or "the demand for motel rooms at the beach per summer season."

As the price of orange juice increases we become less willing to buy ("It's too expensive!") and we look for alternatives such as grapefruit juice, and we become less able to buy ("I can't afford that!"). When the price of a good rises we buy less: when the price falls we buy more. This behavior is summarized in the Law of Demand.

Law of Demand

Simply, the Law of Demand states that there is a negative relationship between two variables, the "price" of a good and "the quantity demanded per time period." "Quantity demanded" is how much the buyer is willing and able to purchase at a single price during some time period. (From now on, for convenience, we'll make the "per time period" phrase implicit.) As "price" changes, "quantity demanded" changes.

This negative relationship can be shown as a demand schedule or as a demand curve (Figure 2-1). This relationship is true whether we are looking at the behavior of an individual buyer or all buyers together. At the level of the market, demand is merely the sum at each price of the demand of individual buyers. By convention, we label our demand curve "D."

A demand schedule is a table showing the "quantity demanded" at each of a number of prices. The following demand schedule shows plausible values for the quantity of apples demanded at a Saturday morning farmer's market at a range of prices.

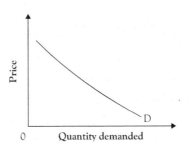

Figure 2-1. A general demand curve relationship.

Table 2-1. A Demand Schedule for Apples

Price of an Apple	Quantity Demanded of Apples
60¢	300
50¢	450
40¢	550
30¢	650
20¢	800
10¢	1000

The table shows that as the price of apples increases, fewer apples are demanded.

The Law of Demand, which states that the two variables ("price" and "quantity demanded") exhibit a negative relationship, can be depicted by a downward-sloping demand curve on a diagram with "price" on the vertical axis and "quantity demanded" on the horizontal axis. The demand curve for apples is plotted in Figure 2-2 as an example.

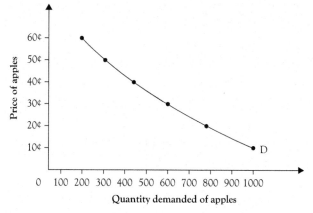

Figure 2-2. The demand curve for apples.

When the price of apples changes from 20¢ to 50¢, it causes a "change in quantity demanded" from 800 apples to down 450 apples, and that this "change in quantity demanded" is shown as a movement along the demand curve in Figure 2-3.

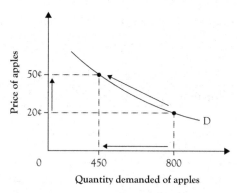

Figure 2-3. A change in quantity demanded.

A **change in quantity demanded** is a movement along the demand curve, and it is caused by a change in the price of the good. The ONLY thing that can cause a change in quantity demanded is a change in the price of the good.

Comment: "But," you object, "surely there are factors other than the price of apples that affect how many apples are demanded!" You are correct. We'll resolve this apparent paradox soon; however, now is a convenient point at which we introduce and discuss modeling.

Modeling and the *ceteris paribus* assumption: We wish to construct a model of how buyers and sellers operate within markets and, within such an environment, many things could be happening at the same time. Such a buzz of activity may make it difficult to isolate a particular factor that we'd like to study—imagine trying to isolate the playing of the third violin in a large orchestra. Models are formal statements of relationships between variables of interest that simplify and abstract from reality. They can be in the form of graphs, words, or equations. Scientists try to simplify by imposing order by factoring out distracting real-world details—chemists, for example, assume the experiments are conducted at a standard temperature and pressure. Physicists may assume that a body in motion is frictionless even when it isn't. When testing a model (for example, the relationship between the price of a good and quantity demanded of that good), it is convenient to assume that all other variables have been held constant. This is the *ceteris paribus* assumption, sometimes expressed as "all else remaining equal."

Supply

We can define **supply** as the willingness and ability to produce (and make available for sale) a quantity of a good or service at a range of prices during some time period. To be part of the supply of a good we must be both willing and able to bring the good to market. A producer who keeps his or her output in a warehouse is not counted as part of supply. As with demand, we have written a time frame into our definition. When we talk about "the supply for Honda Civics" or "the supply of oil" we should have some time period in mind.

As the price of orange juice increases, we become more willing to produce (higher rewards increase motivation) and we become more able to produce (higher revenues allow us to hire more resources). When the price of a good rises we supply more: when the price falls we supply less. This behavior is summarized in the Law of Supply.

Law of Supply

Simply, the Law of Supply states that there is a positive relationship between two variables, the "price" of a good and "the quantity supplied per time period." "Quantity supplied" is how much the seller is willing and able to produce and make available at a single price during some time period. (Again, for convenience, we'll make the "per time period" phrase implicit.) As "price" changes, "quantity supplied" changes.

This positive relationship can be shown as a supply schedule or as a supply curve (Figure 2-4). This relationship is true whether we are looking at the behavior of an individual firm or all firms together. At the level of the market, supply is merely the sum at each price of the supply of individual producers. By convention, we label our supply curve "S."

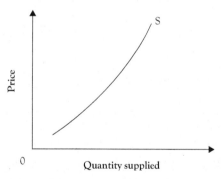

Figure 2-4. A general supply curve relationship.

A supply schedule is a table showing the "quantity supplied" at each of a number of prices. The following supply schedule shows plausible values for the quantity of apples supplied at a Saturday morning farmer's market at a range of prices.

Table 2-2. A Supply Schedule for Apples

Price of an Apple	Quantity Supplied of Apples
60¢	700
50¢	650
40¢	550
30¢	450
20¢	300
10¢	200

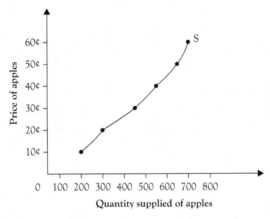

Figure 2-5. The supply curve for apples.

The table shows that as the price of apples increases, more apples are made available for sale.

The Law of Supply states that the two variables ("price" and "quantity supplied") exhibit a positive relationship. This relationship can be depicted by an upward-sloping supply curve on a diagram with "price" on the vertical axis and "quantity supplied" on the horizontal axis. As an example, the supply curve for apples is plotted in Figure 2-5.

When the price of apples changes from 20¢ to 50¢, there is a "change in quantity supplied" from 300 apples to 650 apples, and that this "change in quantity supplied" is shown as a movement along the supply curve in Figure 2-6.

A **change in quantity supplied** is a movement along the supply curve, and it is caused by a change in the price of the good. The ONLY

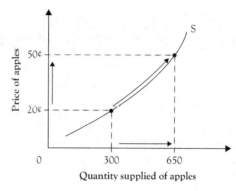

Figure 2-6. A change in quantity supplied.

thing that can cause a change in quantity supplied is a change in the price of the good.

Comment: As with the earlier assertion that a "change in quantity demanded" can only be caused by a change in the price of the good, you may object that other factors may affect how many apples farmers will market. This is correct. Again, we must wait to resolve this apparent paradox.

Modeling the Market

We can now examine how participants interact in a market. The following Table 2-3 and Figure 2-7 combine the previous demand and supply schedules.

When the price is 60¢ per apple, quantity supplied exceeds quantity demanded, and there is a **surplus** of 400 apples (700 – 300). A surplus occurs when quantity demanded is less than quantity supplied. When there is a surplus, there is a downward pressure on price. In an effort to sell the unwanted apples, sellers will reduce the price. If the price decreases to 50¢, the same result occurs—a surplus and a downward pressure on price. Note that, as the price decreases, quantity demanded increases from 300 to 450. This is shown in Figure 2-7 as a movement along the demand curve. Similarly, as the price decreases, some producers will withdraw apples from sale, causing the quantity of apples supplied to decrease from 700 to 650. This is shown as a movement along the supply curve.

A **shortage** occurs when quantity demanded exceeds quantity supplied. When there is a shortage, there is an upward pressure on price.

Table 2-3. Adjustment to equilibrium

Price	Quantity Demanded	Quantity Supplied	Result	Price Pressure
60¢	300	700	surplus	downward
50¢	450	650	surplus	downward
40¢	550	550	equilibrium	none
30¢	650	450	shortage	upward
20¢	800	300	shortage	upward
10¢	1000	200	shortage	upward

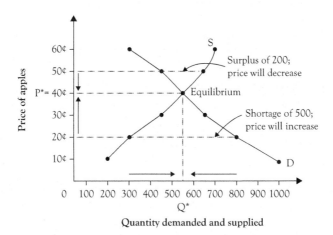

Figure 2-7. Adjustment to equilibrium.

Suppose the price tumbles to 10¢ per apples. Quantity demanded (1,000 apples) exceeds quantity supplied (200 apples), and there will be a shortage of 800 apples. Buyers, some of whom are willing to pay 60¢ or more and are desperate to secure apples, will bid up the price. As price rises, quantity demanded will decrease and quantity supplied will increase until the shortage is competed away until equilibrium is established. **Equilibrium** occurs at the price level where quantity demanded equals quantity supplied. The equilibrium price (P*) is 40¢ and the equilibrium quantity (Q*) is 550 apples. When the market is in equilibrium, there is no pressure for the price to change and, at this price, all buyers and sellers in the market are receiving an acceptable outcome.

Prices are a signaling and rationing mechanism in markets. When the quantity demanded of apples exceeds quantity supplied, a shortage is present and we would expect the price of apples to increase. The rise in the price of apples signals to apple growers that more resources should be allocated to the production of apples. At the same time, the rise in price encourages some potential buyers of apples to look elsewhere for alternatives (such as pears) and the apples that are available are channeled to those who are most willing and able to pay for them.

Caution: The assumption being made at this point is that those who buy the apples value them more highly than those who are priced out of the market. You might wish to consider whether this is always true!

What's so Great About Equilibrium?

To this point, we have developed a model of how a market reflects the wishes of buyers and sellers and establishes equilibrium. Markets achieve equilibrium where quantity demanded equals quantity supplied. With this result, all of the market participants receive an outcome with which they are satisfied. In fact, society's overall satisfaction is maximized (as we shall see in the next chapter).

Factors that can shift the position of the demand curve causing a "change in demand." Although price is an important element in determining willingness and ability to purchase, it is certainly not the only factor. In terms of Figure 2-8, consumers of apples may decide that, at any price, they want more apples than they did before. In Figure 2-8, this greater demand for apples would be shown as a

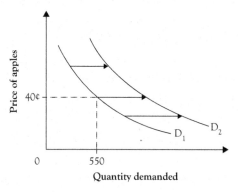

Figure 2-8. An increase in demand.

rightward shift of the demand curve from D_1 to D_2 and would be termed an **increase in demand**. If demand decreases, then the curve would shift over to the left.

Numerous factors may shift the position of a demand curve for a good, but to keep our model manageable we will restrict ourselves to a short list of the major factors, including changes in tastes and preferences, after-tax income or wealth, expectations about price, income or wealth, the prices of related products, and the number or composition of buyers.

Tastes and preferences: As goods come into style or fall out of fashion, demand shifts. If apples become more popular, perhaps because of new advertising claims emphasizing health benefits of an "apple a day," then, even at the same price, more apples would be demanded and the demand curve would shift to the right. The demand for ice cream will increase on a hot summer day; the demand for leaf blowers is lower in the spring than in the fall; the demand for wrapping paper increases in December.

THINK IT THROUGH: Come up with at least one real-world example of both an increase in demand and a decrease in demand in response to a change in tastes and preferences.

After-tax income or wealth: As our spending power increases, we buy more. Research has shown that a 10 percent increase in disposable income will cause a 24 percent increase in the demand for automobiles, a 14 percent increase in the demand for restaurant meals, and a 5 percent increase in the demand for oil and gasoline products. This is the response we see for a **normal good**—higher income, higher demand; lower income, lower demand.

Conceptually, wealth differs from income (a wealthy person may have no income this year but still remain wealthy), but the relationship with demand is similar. As wealth increases, the demand for normal goods increases. The burgeoning consumer spending during the 1990s was due, in part, to the steep rise in the values of stock market portfolios while much of the clampdown in consumer spending at the start of the Great Recession was, similarly, due to the slashing reductions in the value of consumers' financial and property assets.

Most, but not all goods, though, react this way. Some goods are **inferior goods**. The demand for "inferior" goods decreases as consumers become more affluent and increases when the household's fortunes turn downwards. Ramen noodles, beans and rice, and bologna are examples. Can you think of examples of goods that you would demand more if you lost your job? During the Great Recession there was a boom in the demand for bankruptcy lawyers, condoms, and community college courses.

THINK IT THROUGH: Come up with at least one real-world example of both a normal good and an inferior good.

Expectations about price, income, or wealth: If we expect the price of a good to increase, we'll tend to buy more today. If, though, we hear news that a good's price will fall soon, then we may try to postpone purchase until after the decrease in price. Note that the price has not yet changed—only the expectation that the price may change.

Similarly, demand can be affected by expectations about income or wealth. If credible rumors circulate through your firm that there soon will be layoffs, or if you expect adverse effects on your retirement plan, then this new information will affect your purchasing behavior—demand for normal goods will decrease but demand for inferior goods will increase. A threatened redundancy may lead you to shelve plans for that European vacation (a normal good) and choose to stay home and plant a vegetable garden (an inferior good) instead.

If income or wealth is expected to increase, then the demand for normal goods will increase and the demand for inferior goods will decrease. College students tend to spend more freely and incur debt (student loans and credit cards) because, although they are poor now, they expect to be prosperous after graduation. Expectations make students a prime target for lenders.

THINK IT THROUGH: Find at least one real-world example of a good (a normal good) whose demand would increase if you expected your income or wealth to increase and one real-world example of a good (an inferior good) whose demand would increase if you expected your income or wealth to decrease.

Prices of related products: **Substitutes** are goods that are alternatives for each other—Exxon gasoline or BP. Many goods are substitutes for each other—some are close substitutes (Coca-Cola and Pepsi), some are more distant (Coca-Cola and Snapple).

Other goods may be complements for each other. **Complements** are goods that tend to be used together. Tennis balls and tennis racquets, CD players and batteries, cat food and kitty litter are all examples of complementary pairs of goods. Driving your car involves a mass of goods that are consumed at the same time—gasoline, oil, tires, insurance and so on.

Note that substitutes or complements need not be purchased at the same time or at the same rate, merely that the demand for one affects the demand for the other.

THINK IT THROUGH: Find at least one real-world example of two goods that are substitutes and two goods that are complements.

Note: For convenience, from now on we will abbreviate "Price" to "P" and "Quantity" to "Q" in our figures.

Given two substitutes (Coke and Pepsi, for example), if the price of Coke increases P_1 to P_2, then this will cause a decrease in the quantity demanded of Coke (a movement along the demand curve for Coke from Q_1 to Q_2). We will look around for alternatives such as Pepsi. More shoppers than before will demand Pepsi, even although the price of Pepsi (P) has not changed. The demand curve for Pepsi will shift to the right from D_1 to D_2 because of the increase in the price of Coke. See Figure 2-9.

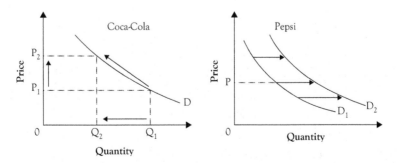

Figure 2-9. The relationship between substitutes.

THINK IT THROUGH: Verify this result that the demand for Good B will increase if the price of substitute Good A increases, using your own example of two substitute goods. Can you also construct the argument if the price of Good A decreases instead?

Given two complements (peanut butter and jelly, for example), if the price of peanut butter increases from P_1 to P_2 then this will cause a decrease in the quantity demanded of peanut butter (a movement along the demand curve for peanut butter from Q_1 to Q_2 as we would expect from the Law of Demand). Because we use peanut butter and jelly together and we're buying less peanut butter, then we'll buy less jelly too, even although the price of jelly (P) has not changed. The demand curve for jelly will shift to the left from D_1 to D_2 because of the increase in the price of peanut butter. See Figure 2-10.

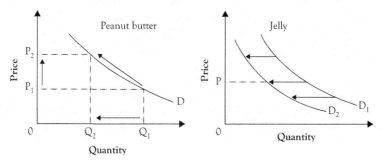

Figure 2-10. The relationship between complements.

THINK IT THROUGH: Verify this result that the demand for Good B will decrease if the price of complementary Good A increases, using your own example of two complements. Can you also construct the argument if the price of Good A decreases instead?

Number or composition of buyers: If more buyers enter a market, we'd expect the demand for a product to increase. For instance, on the one hand, if the legal drinking age were reduced to sixteen, then the demand for beer would increase; on the other hand, Prohibition would reduce the demand for alcohol. The demand for eBay and other online goods would increase with greater Internet access.

On the one hand, the demand for anti-wrinkle creams, gyms, and Rogaine will increase as the population ages; on the other hand, a young (child-bearing) population will experience increased demand for diapers, bassinets, toys, and car seats for children.

THINK IT THROUGH: Again, devise your own intuitive examples of situations where changes in the number and composition of buyers would influence demand.

Factors that can shift the position of the supply curve causing a "change in supply." Although price is an important factor in determining willingness and ability to produce, other factors are important too. In terms of Figure 2-11, apple growers may decide that, at any price, they wish to produce more apples than they did previously. In Figure 2-11, the greater supply of apples is shown as a rightward shift of the supply curve from S_1 to S_2 and would be called as an "increase in supply." If supply decreases, then the curve would shift over to the left.

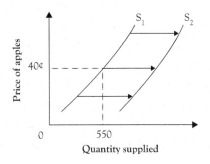

Figure 2-11. An increase in supply.

Caution: As noted earlier, although we say "demand has gone up" and "supply has gone down," demand and supply curves should be thought of as moving left and right on the figure, not vertically up and down.

Numerous factors may shift the position of a supply curve for a good but, as with demand, to keep our model manageable we will restrict ourselves to a short list of the major factors, including changes in technology, productivity, the price of inputs, after-tax revenues, the prices of related products in production, and the number of sellers.

Learning Tip: Be aware that most students find supply more difficult to grasp than demand—we're more used to thinking of ourselves as consumers. When thinking about how the supply curve shifts, keep in mind the phrase "Follow the profit!" If something happens (other than a change in price), will it directly affect profit? If profit increases as a consequence of the change then supply will increase (shift to the right); if profit decreases then supply will decrease (shift to the left).

Price of inputs: If the price of inputs (for example, workers' wages, the price of fuel, and the salaries of executives) increases then profitability will decrease and supply will be reduced. A decrease in input prices will have the opposite effect.

THINK IT THROUGH: Verify the effect that an increase in the minimum wage will have on production in an industry that depends on minimum-wage workers. Recall the *ceteris paribus* assumption—there is no expectation that workers will "work harder" just because their wages have been increased.

Technology: An improvement in technology will decrease costs of production, increase profit, and cause an increase in supply. Examples include a more effective floor plan for the factory or a cheaper storage/distribution system. It's hard to imagine a situation where a technology would be adopted that would knowingly cause a decrease in profit, but, if this happened, then the supply curve would shift to the left. An example of choosing inferior technology might be anti-pollution regulations forcing the adoption of a "greener" but less cost-effective method of production.

Caution: Just because there is a technological improvement in the method of production of a good, it should not be taken to mean that the product itself has been improved. That is quite a different issue. As consumers, we don't know or care much about the methods used to produce the goods we buy.

THINK IT THROUGH: Find an example of a technological improvement (perhaps from your own experience) and demonstrate that, at the same price as before, because costs are reduced and profits are increased, producers will be more able and willing to increase output.

Productivity: If workers become more productive then the unit costs of production will be decreased, profitability will increase, and producers will be able to expand output. Note that we are assuming that the increase in productivity is not caused by an increase in wages nor, in turn, does it cause an increase in wages. A decrease in productivity (perhaps a new law mandating longer breaks for workers or more frequent inspections of machines) would decrease productivity and drive the supply curve to the left.

THINK IT THROUGH: Again, devise your own intuitive example of a situation where productivity has increased and determine the effect on supply.

After-tax revenues: An increase in taxes on producers will reduce revenues and reduce supply. An excise tax levied on gasoline, for example, will increase the price of gasoline because supply has been reduced. A reduction in such a tax will have the opposite effect. A subsidy is almost like a "negative" tax—a tax takes money away while a subsidy bestows money. A new subsidy (or an increase in an existing one) will increase profitability and prompt a greater supply.

THINK IT THROUGH: Separate from the government's need to collect revenues, "sin" taxes are imposed on cigarettes, wine, and spirits, and gasoline in order to discourage production and consumption of such "bad" goods. For many years, a honey subsidy was part of the Agriculture Bill because pollination by bees was felt to be beneficial for agriculture in general. The subsidy increased the supply of honey and the pollinating services of the bees.

THINK IT THROUGH: Apart from the examples given, can you think of other examples of "sin" taxes? Also, what would happen to supply of, for example, beer if the government increased corporate income taxes?

Prices of related products in production: We included the price of related goods (substitutes and complements) among the factors that could shift the position of a demand curve. The same is true for supply—but we must be careful! Just because two goods are, for instance, complements for consumers does not guarantee that they will also be complements for producers. For the Smith family, a wooden table and four wooden chairs are complements—the family will buy the table and chairs to use them together. However, for the furniture producer, the table takes up resources that could be used to produce chairs—tables and chairs are substitutes in production. As we can see from this example, it is unwise to assume that, because Good A and Good B are substitutes (or complements) for consumers, they must therefore have any particular relationship from the standpoint of producers.

To make this issue a little clearer, let's adopt the practice of referring to two goods that are substitutes on the supply side as **substitutes in production** and to two goods that are complements on the supply side as **complements in production**.

Consider a farmer who can produce soybeans or corn. If the price of corn increases from P_1 to P_2, then the Law of Supply tells us that the farmer will devote more of his or her resources to the production of corn and, therefore, less of those resources will be devoted to the production of soybeans. Soybean production will decrease from S_1 to S_2 at every price level. Corn and soybeans are substitutes in production and when the price of one of the goods increases, then the supply of the other good will decrease. See Figure 2-12.

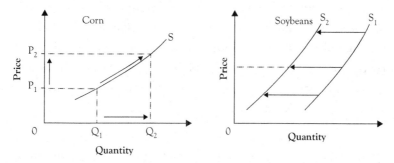

Figure 2-12. The relationship between substitutes in production.

Although goods are most likely to be substitutes in production because they are in competition for the firm's resources, it is possible that two goods may be complements in production. This case occurs when two goods are produced together, usually with one being a by-product of the other. Beef and hides are the standard textbook example of a pair of goods that are complements in production. Other examples include natural gas and helium; mutton and wool; doughnuts and doughnut holes; and ethanol and high-protein corn mash for cattle.

The production of milk requires pregnant cows. If the price of milk increases from P_1 to P_2, then there will be an increase in the quantity of milk supplied (from Q_1 to Q_2) due to an increase in bovine pregnancies

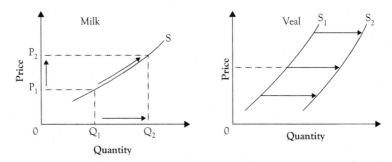

Figure 2-13. The relationship between complements in production.

and deliveries. There will, in short, be more calves born. About half of these calves will be non-milk-producing males so, because of the increase in the price of milk, there will be an increase in the supply of veal from S_1 to S_2. See Figure 2-13. Milk and veal are complements in production.

THINK IT THROUGH: Find at least one real-world example of two goods that are substitutes in production and two goods that are complements in production.

Number of sellers: We assume that as more firms enter an industry there will be greater supply. With more restaurants in town, the supply of restaurant meals will increase. If, by contrast, the number of plumbers in town is halved (perhaps because of a new regulation requiring certification), then the supply of plumbing services will be reduced.

Applying Demand and Supply Analysis

Single-Shift Cases

We can now apply the tool we have developed by considering the beer industry. Suppose we are given four snippets of information about circumstances in the beer industry and asked to predict their consequences. The four pieces of information are:

> Case 1. Beer has been proved conclusively to increase male sexual performance.
> Case 2. Wine has become much less expensive than before.

Case 3. There has been a very large harvest of hops. (Hops are an ingredient in the production of beer.)

Case 4. Beer workers have negotiated a ten percent increase in their wages.

We will treat each of these situations separately. First, think about each situation. Jot down in the following table what you think will happen, as a consequence of this shock to the market, to the price of beer (increase or decrease), and to the size of the beer market (increase or decrease). We'll check your predictions later.

	Effect on Price	Effect on Quantity
Case 1	_____	_____
Case 2	_____	_____
Case 3	_____	_____
Case 4	_____	_____

As in many areas of life, it is useful to have a style of approach when dealing with demand and supply analysis. First, make it a habit to sketch a demand and supply diagram as in Figure 2-14, with "price" (P) on the vertical axis and "quantity" (Q) on the horizontal axis. Draw in a downward-sloping demand curve and label it D_1 then an upward-sloping supply curve and label it S_1. We know that equilibrium occurs where the two lines cross so we can draw in the equilibrium price level (P*) and the equilibrium quantity (Q*). We now have a representation of the beer market as it stands at the beginning of the analysis.

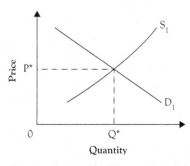

Figure 2-14. The initial equilibrium diagram.

Learning Tip: Once you've identified that you're dealing with a demand and supply problem, always sketch your initial diagram like this before you continue. It's easier to identify the initial equilibrium price and quantity before you start shifting lines back and forth.

Case 1: Beer has been proved conclusively to
          increase male sexual performance

The first question to answer is "Will this market shock affect the demand for beer or the supply of beer?" The instinctive but almost certainly incorrect answer is "Both!" We have a list of factors that can shift the position of the demand curve and another list of factors that can shift the position of the supply curve. Which factor on which list best fits this situation?

Certainly there will be a change in demand (tastes and preferences) following this information—isn't that what advertising is all about? In each case, you should be able to identify the category of factor that is causing the change in demand (or supply).

The second question to address is "Will demand—because now we've determined it is a demand change—increase or decrease?" It's a safe bet in this situation of promised enhanced sexual performance that the demand for beer will increase. The demand curve will shift to the right.

Draw the demand curve in its new position (D_2). We know that equilibrium occurs where the demand curve and the supply curve cross. Draw in the new equilibrium price level (P^{**}) and the new equilibrium quantity (Q^{**}) on your diagram. Price has increased and quantity has increased. See Figure 2-15.

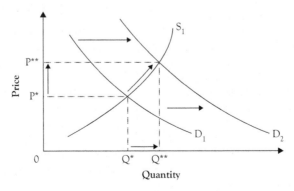

Figure 2-15. An increase in demand.

A successful advertising campaign or the discovery of a new use for an existing product will cause an increase in its price and an increase in the size of the market. Is this the result you predicted?

"Not so fast!" you exclaim. "Won't supply increase too? Why is 'both' an incorrect response?" Typically, the predominant effect will fall on only one side of the market so, although it sometimes may be true that a market shock will affect the positions of both curves, the "both" response is usually the result of misthinking. Removing the "both" response forces a considered choice.

False logic: It is also true that more beer will be supplied, but this is not because of an increase in supply. It's an "increase in quantity supplied" in response to the initial change in demand. The cause-and-effect sequence goes like this: The increase in demand causes a shortage at the initial equilibrium price (P*) and the shortage pressures the price to increase. As the price of beer increases, the "quantity supplied of beer" increases—this is a movement along the existing supply curve, not a shift in the position of the curve—and decreases the "quantity demanded of beer" along the new demand curve (D_2).

In summary, this market shock makes only the demand curve shift.

A useful rule to remember is: "One factor shifts one curve and it shifts it only one time."

A note on the difference between a "change in demand" and a inverted commas quantity demanded": The one major source of confusion in a Principles of Economics course is the distinction between a "change in quantity demanded" and a "change in demand." Beware! These two terms have very precise meanings in economics.

A "change in quantity demanded" refers to a movement along a demand curve, from one point to another. The only thing that can cause a change in quantity demanded is a change in the price of the good. The only thing! A "change in demand" refers to a shift (left or right) in the position of the demand curve. If income, the price of a substitute, tastes and preferences (and so on) change, then the demand curve must be redrawn—a change in demand. Although this might sound easy enough, it causes endless confusion even for the most diligent student.

Remember: A change in price causes a "change in quantity demanded," which is a movement along the curve. A change in some other factor causes a "change in demand," which is a movement of the entire demand curve.

Case 2. Wine has become much less expensive than before

As in Case 1, we must answer two questions: "Will this market shock affect the demand for beer or the supply of beer?" and "Will it be an increase or a decrease?" For most beer drinkers, wine is an acceptable substitute, so cheaper wine will have an impact on the demand for beer. In fact, if the price of wine has decreased, the demand for beer will decrease. The demand curve will shift to the left.

Draw the demand curve in its new position (D_2). Equilibrium price decreases from P* to P** and equilibrium quantity decreases from Q* to Q**. See Figure 2-16.

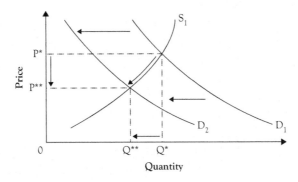

Figure 2-16. A decrease in demand.

THINK IT THROUGH: Verify that this result makes sense to you. Does it square with your prediction? If not, why not?

Case 3. There has been a very large harvest of hops
        (Hops are an ingredient in the production of beer.)

Will this market shock affect the demand for beer or the supply of beer? Unless the quality of the hops has changed, affecting the taste of the beer,

beer drinkers are unlikely to care about hop yields. This is a production side issue and supply will increase. There's a brief explanation for this—more ingredients, more beer! We can be more subtle than that. With a large harvest of hops, the price of hops will decrease so the price of an input has decreased. Follow the profit! With lower costs, profitability will increase, leading to an increase in supply. The supply curve will shift to the right.

Draw the supply curve in its new position (S$_2$). Equilibrium price decreases from P* to P** and equilibrium quantity increases from Q* to Q**. See Figure 2-17.

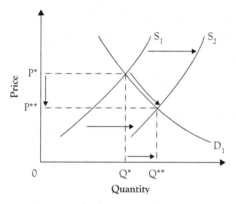

Figure 2-17. An increase in supply.

THINK IT THROUGH: Does this result—that a large hop harvest is great news for beer drinkers—make sense to you? Does it match your prediction? If not, why not?

Case 4. Beer workers have negotiated a ten percent
        increase in their wages

Will the wage increase affect the demand for beer or the supply of beer? Beer workers may be beer drinkers, but the predominant effect is on the costs of producing beer. Following our "one factor shifts one curve" rule, it's the supply curve that will be affected. Follow the profit! With higher costs, profitability will be reduced, leading to a cutback in supply. The supply curve will shift to the left.

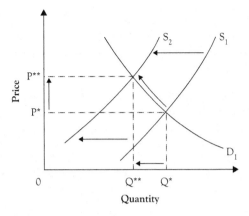

Figure 2-18. A decrease in supply.

Draw the supply curve in its new position (S$_2$). Equilibrium price increases from P* to P** and equilibrium quantity decreases from Q* to Q**. See Figure 2-18.

THINK IT THROUGH: Does this result make sense to you? Higher wage payments should drive up prices and cause layoffs in the beer industry. Does it match your prediction? If not, why not?

Review: There are four single-shift cases. Either demand increases or decreases, or supply increases or decreases. The following table summarizes the results we have found and should agree with the predictions that you made earlier.

	Effect on Price	Effect on Quantity
Demand Increase	increase	increase
Demand Decrease	decrease	decrease
Supply Increase	decrease	increase
Supply Decrease	increase	decrease

Multiple-Shift Cases: It is possible that two shocks could hit a market at the same time. Suppose we are given two pieces of information about circumstances in the market for domestically produced wine and asked to predict their consequences. The two pieces of information are that import taxes on foreign wine have been reduced and that improved fermenting techniques have reduced the costs of wine production.

Initially, we will deal with this as two "single-shift" cases.

If import taxes on foreign wine have been reduced, then this will reduce the demand for domestically produced wine because the price of the substitute will have decreased. Adopting improved fermentation processes techniques should reduce production costs and increase the supply of domestically produced wine. Because we have a decrease in demand (which will decrease price) and an increase in supply (which also will decrease price), we would predict unambiguously that the price of domestically produced wine will decrease. However, we can't be so sure about the effect of the two shocks on quantity. We have a decrease in demand (which will decrease quantity) and an increase in supply (which will increase quantity) therefore the overall effect on quantity is indeterminate unless we know something more specific about the magnitude of the shifts in demand and supply.

THINK IT THROUGH: Try drawing this example. As always, begin with the initial equilibrium diagram (Figure 2-14), including the initial equilibrium price (P*) and quantity (Q*). Verify that the effect on equilibrium quantity depends on the magnitudes of the two conflicting shifts.

THINK IT THROUGH: Come up with an example where two shocks cause an ambiguous result, not for equilibrium quantity, but for equilibrium price.

Review: This has been a long, arduous chapter dealing, as it does, with the primary tool of economists—demand and supply. The single best piece of advice is "practice, practice, practice" and, with respect to diagrams, "draw, draw, draw." The slippery distinction between a "change in quantity demanded" (caused by a change in price and shown as a movement along an existing demand curve) and a "change in demand" (caused by other factors and shown as a shift in the position of the demand curve) is controlled if a diagram is drawn. Like any tool, demand and supply analysis requires repeated practice before there is any sense of perfection but it is worth the effort because the tool is so generally applicable in the real world.

CHAPTER 3

More on Markets

By the end of this chapter you will be able to:

1. Distinguish between marginal utility and total utility.
2. State the law of diminishing marginal utility and relate it to the downward-sloping demand curve.
3. State the utility-maximizing rule in words and mathematically, and analyze how the consumer would respond to disequilibrium situations.
4. Relate the utility-maximizing rule to the diamond/water paradox.
5. Distinguish between the substitution effect and the income effect and use them to explain the slope of the demand curve.
6. Define marginal benefit and consumer surplus and relate them to the demand curve.
7. Define marginal cost and producer surplus and relate them to the supply curve.
8. Relate consumer surplus and producer surplus to allocative efficiency.
9. Define price ceiling and price floor and explain their effects on market efficiency.

Prices operate to ration the goods and services we consume—and usually ration rather well. This is why it is dangerous to go to an all-you-can-eat restaurant! As we shall see in this chapter, once you have paid for your meal, the economics are against you as you risk losing the rationing discipline imposed by the market.

Chapter Preview: In Chapter 2 we discovered how markets achieve equilibrium and how they respond to changes in demand and supply conditions. Although many economists feel that market forces should be permitted to determine the economy's output mix and price structure, very few would assert that no intervention in markets is ever justified. In this chapter, we learn more about how and why markets are controlled and some of the consequences of such controls. We also look more closely at why economists feel so strongly that, left to their own devices, markets generally do a good job of allocating the economy's scarce resources.

First, however, we examine the theoretical basis underlying the negatively sloped demand curve. We know, intuitively, that higher prices choke off consumer enthusiasm. But why?

Brain Teaser: In 1776, Adam Smith's *Wealth of Nations* popularized a classic economics puzzle—the diamond/water paradox. Smith noted that, for most of us, diamonds have only slight practical value, but are prized (and priced) much more highly than water, which is essential for life. Can you puzzle out the reason for this apparent discrepancy before we reach the explanation later in this chapter?

Demand Revisited

Explanations for the Negative Relationship

Nineteenth-century economists had stated the Law of Demand and drawn a demand curve showing the intuitive relationship between the price of a good and the quantity of the good demanded. They then turned to the task of finding an explanation for the relationship they had described. Throughout the years, several alternative models have been put forward to explain why we tend to buy less of a good when the price of the good increases. One of the earliest attempts is known as Utility Theory, and it produced several useful insights including the Law of Diminishing Marginal Utility and the Utility-Maximizing Rule.

Utility Theory

Utility is the term used by economists to mean satisfaction or enjoyment. A good or an experience provides satisfaction—it provides utility. Note that a good need not be "useful" in the practical sense to provide utility— a beautiful painting may have no practical use but it may still give us enjoyment. Leisure also provides utility.

The **Law of Diminishing Marginal Utility** states that, after some point, equal successive units of a good consumed will yield diminishing marginal utility. This brings us to two points that must be addressed before we can proceed: What is marginal utility, and how can we measure it?

What is marginal utility and how can we measure it?

Answering the second question first—we can't! We can't, at least in the direct sense that we can measure weight, or temperature, or even intelligence. However, we can measure it indirectly as we do know that a chilled can of Coca-Cola after a hot afternoon of yard work certainly gives us some enjoyment. We also know that, if there are two cans—perhaps a can of Sprite and the can of Coke—then, if we choose the Coke, it's because the Coke bestows more utility than the Sprite.

In the early days, economists were hopeful that some sort of utility measurement could be devised—one that was reliable and allowed comparisons between people—but this has been proven to be a false hope. However, by choosing the Coke over the Sprite, our actions reveal our preferences and offer some glimpse of the utility being offered by the two sodas. Later economists have minted the fictitious unit, the "util," to measure utility. Our discussion of utility follows this tradition.

Marginal utility is the additional utility derived from an additional unit of a good consumed. **Total utility** is the sum of these additional contributions to your level of satisfaction. Think about a bag of potato chips. Lay's currently has a slogan—"Bet you can't eat just one!"—and, while that may be true, eventually, you will stop eating the chips, either by reaching the bottom of the bag or by turning to other attractions. The first few potato chips may provide quite significant increases in your total utility (the taste, the salt), but subsequent chips are likely to contribute progressively less additional utility—as your hunger decreases and your guilt increases. You are experiencing diminishing marginal utility—subsequent units yield less additional satisfaction than earlier units do.

If an extra item adds nothing to your overall level of satisfaction, then marginal utility has become zero. Put differently, total utility is maximized when marginal utility is zero. Marginal utility can even be negative—if an extra item is actually distasteful to you, although one would wonder about the circumstances surrounding the consumption of such a good.

THINK IT THROUGH: Here is the answer to the question posed at the beginning of the chapter regarding the all-you-can-eat restaurant. The diner maximizes his or her utility by eating until the point where the marginal utility of the last mouthful is zero. Rising from the table before that point incurs a reduction in utility that may be difficult to resist. If the individual were offered access to a free mini-bar, similar overindulgence may occur. Paying as you go reduces such temptation.

The relationship between marginal utility and total utility is shown in the following example concerning Adam's consumption of slices of pizza. Prior to his meal, we assume Adam has received no satisfaction from pizza consumption. The first slice adds 15 utils of satisfaction, making his total utility 15 utils. Given the law of diminishing marginal utility, we would expect that the second slice would yield less additional satisfaction than the first, with total utility increasing to 28 utils. Complete Table 3-1.

Total utility increases to 38 utils with the third slice of pizza because the extra satisfaction from that slice must be 10 utils. The fourth slice adds 7 utils, making the total utility 45 utils. The fifth slice raises the total utility (by 5 utils) to 50 utils. The sixth slice adds 3 utils to make Adam's total utility 63 utils.

Mathematical Note: At more advanced levels of economics, total utility can be described by a mathematical equation—a total utility function.

Table 3-1. Total Utility and Marginal Utility

Number of Slices	Total Utility	Marginal Utility
1	15	15
2	28	13
3	38	
4		7
5	50	
6		3

Marginal utility is the derivative of the total utility function. This relationship is also present for other "total-marginal" pairs in economics, such as total revenue and marginal revenue, total cost and marginal cost, and total benefit and marginal benefit.

THINK IT THROUGH: When Mick Jagger famously sang "I can't get no satisfaction," was he referring to his total utility or to his marginal utility? Assuming away the double negative in the lyrics, Jagger (who attended the London School of Economics) must have been meaning marginal utility, as it is unlikely that his total level of enjoyment in life was zero.

THINK IT THROUGH MORE: If, indeed, Jagger is referring to marginal utility, then what does his assertion tell us about the level of his total utility? If he has reached the point where his marginal utility is zero, then his total utility must be maximized.

THINK IT THROUGH: The Law of Diminishing Marginal Utility states that, after some point, equal successive units of a good consumed will yield diminishing marginal utility. This does not rule out the possibility that, initially, marginal utility could increase as equal additional units are consumed. Can you think of any examples of increasing marginal utility? Examples might include activities where satisfaction increases with skill or heightened appreciation. Repeated listens to a piece of music might enhance enjoyment.

THINK IT THROUGH: If we experience diminishing marginal utility from the dollars we receive as income, does it make sense to redistribute income from rich people to poor people? At the societal level, because the utility lost from the dollar taken from the rich person presumably would be less than the utility gained from the same dollar given to the poor person, then society would gain from the redistribution.

THINK IT THROUGH MORE: Should we reallocate so that everyone's income is equal? No. For one thing, the assumption that "because dollars are equalized then marginal utilities must be equalized" is questionable. Also, what about incentives? If we adopt an "equal shares for all" strategy, then the motivation to produce is lessened. If the size of the economic pie is reduced, then we all lose.

The Utility-Maximizing Rule: We can develop a principle to enable the individual to maximize his total utility, given his income, tastes and preferences, and the prices of the goods he might purchase. Simply put, this rule states that the consumer should seek to allocate expenditures and buy goods in such a way that the marginal utility per dollar for the last unit of each good bought is equalized. Mathematically, this would be expressed as

$$MU_A/P_A = MU_B/P_B$$

where MU_A is the marginal utility of the final apple bought, P_A is the price of apples, MU_B is the marginal utility of the final banana bought, and P_B is the price of bananas. All this equation says is that, to get the most satisfaction from one's money, the "extra benefit per dollar" must be equalized for all goods purchased.

Perhaps the easiest way to understand this point is to consider an imbalance in the utility-maximizing condition, for example,

$$MU_A/P_A > MU_B/P_B$$

Example: Joan plans to buy two goods—apples and bananas. The price of each apple is $2.00 and the price of each banana is $1.00. Assuming that Joan receives 30 utils from the final apple purchased and 40 utils from the final banana purchased, we get

$$30/1 > 40/2$$

The marginal utility per dollar for apples is higher than the marginal utility per dollar for bananas—apples are the better deal. Note that this is still true despite the fact that the marginal utility of bananas is higher than the marginal utility of apples. What is important is the "marginal utility per dollar" comparison! even although Joan likes bananas more, in order to get the best "bang for her buck," she should reallocate her expenditure, buying more of the good giving the greater marginal utility per dollar (apples) and less of the other (bananas). This reallocation will remove the imbalance because, as more apples are bought, the marginal utility of the final apple purchased will decrease while, simultaneously, as fewer bananas are bought, the marginal utility of the final banana purchased will increase.

Comment: We catch ourselves indulging in this sort of behavior all the time. In a restaurant, diners check prices before deciding on their order. We scan gas prices along the highway to get the best deal. In the grocery store, we assess different cuts of meat and the prices charged. Why? To get the most satisfaction from our limited grocery budget. In economics, remember, choices are made at the margin.

Brain Teaser Solution: We can now answer the brain teaser that was posed at the beginning of the chapter. Although water is essential to life, it is abundant and the marginal utility of the last gallon consumed by an individual or household is low. We are, therefore, not willing to pay much for water. Diamonds, by contrast, are highly sought after for their intrinsic appeal, despite having no practical value in most circumstances and, therefore, their marginal utility is substantial. Because of this high marginal utility, we are willing to pay a great deal to acquire diamonds.

Diminishing Marginal Utility and Demand: Because marginal utility typically decreases as extra units are consumed, each additional unit can be thought of as being worth less to the consumer. Accordingly, in order to be motivated to purchase, the price of additional units must be reduced.

THINK IT THROUGH: Sellers are well aware of this situation and examples of charging progressively lower prices abound in the market place. "Buy the first, and get the second for half price" and frequent buyer discounts are two examples of pricing strategies intended to entice buyers who are experiencing declining marginal utility. Can you think of others?

Although diminishing marginal utility is a reasonable explanation of the negative relationship between price and quantity demanded, as far as it goes, it remains unsatisfactory, partly because of the measurement problems mentioned earlier. Economists found an alternative and powerful explanation for the negatively sloped demand curve in the substitution effect and the income effect.

The Substitution Effect and the Income Effect

Normal Goods: As we saw in Chapter 2, most goods are normal goods, such as Pepsi and, as the price of the good increases, consumers seek substitutes, such as Coca-Cola. This is the **substitution effect**—an increase in the price of a good motivates consumers to seek substitutes, reducing the quantity demanded of Pepsi. There is also an **income effect** of the price increase. As the price of the good rises, the consumer's spending power is reduced, because his or her food dollars can no longer stretch as far as before and this will affect how much of the good is demanded. For a normal good, a decrease in spending power (income) will reduce quantity demanded. For a normal good, therefore, both effects result in a decrease in the quantity demanded of Pepsi as its price increases.

Inferior Goods: The substitution effect for an inferior good is the same as for a normal good, but the income effect is reversed. Consider an inferior good such as bologna. A rise in price of bologna encourages the consumer to seek substitutes, such as other meats—the substitution effect. However, because of the higher price, the consumer is less well off than before and, we know, poorer consumers buy *more* of inferior goods. In this case, the income effect results in more bologna being bought.

For an inferior good, the substitution effect and the income effect are in conflict but we can infer that the substitution effect is the dominant effect because the demand curve for bologna slopes down. In general, the substitution effect (price higher—buy less) is stronger than the income effect (price higher—buy more), so, on balance, quantity demanded falls when price rises.

THINK IT THROUGH: Choose a normal good and verify the results just discussed when the price of the good decreases. You should find that the substitution effect and the income effect go in the same direction (price lower—buy more). Also, choose an inferior good and check that the effects go in opposite directions.

Comment: Even with inferior goods, the substitution effect dominates. Probably because of this, the substitution effect is far easier to understand, the income effect more arcane.

Giffen Goods: Although a theoretical curiosity, Giffen goods offer good practice on the substitution effect and the income effect. A Giffen good (named after Scottish economist Sir Robert Giffen) is one for which the quantity demanded increases as the price increases—the income effect dominates the substitution effect. To be a Giffen good, the product must be inferior, must have very few substitutes, and must absorb a large part of the buyer's budget. Clearly, such a good is difficult to find and most candidates have been found lacking. Giffen suggested corn for bread-making. With few substitutes, the substitution effect would be weak. If bread forms a large part of one's diet, then a price increase would make one less well off and, with a weak substitution effect, the income effect could dominate. Rice, kerosene, and potatoes have been suggested.

THINK IT THROUGH: For an alcoholic, might very cheap moonshine alcohol qualify as a Giffen good?

The substitution effect and income effect together provide a very satisfactory explanation for the behavior of the demand, but they are rather challenging to present graphically. We want an approach that has the strengths of the two previous approaches and is also more generally applicable. That's what we get with marginal benefit.

Marginal Benefit

Have you ever bid at a live auction or on eBay or similar online sites? What does your bid reveal in such an environment? The bid reveals the maximum amount that you are willing to pay for an item. Your maximum bid shows how much value (or benefit) you attach to the good. Your bid, then, reveals the marginal benefit of the item to you. **Marginal benefit**, abbreviated to MB, is the dollar value of an extra unit of a good consumed.

Clearly, marginal benefit is very similar to marginal utility except for the crucial difference that, in the circumstances described, the value of the good can be measured in dollars and cents—a clear improvement over "utils"! The value of the good to different bidders can be compared, for instance. If bidding takes place in the traditional way, the value of the auctioned item to the ultimate winner may not be known—she merely has to bid a little higher than the second-place bidder. In a Dutch auction, the process is reversed as the auctioneer begins with a high asking price, which is reduced in stages until one participant is willing to accept the last stated price and, by so doing, revealing his marginal benefit.

Comment: In the heat of an auction, where only one bidder can win, one may be tempted to bid a higher amount than the item is worth, and then regret the decision when payment falls due. This is called "buyer's remorse."

A New Way to Look at Demand: Usually when we look at a demand curve, we read it from the vertical axis (price) to the horizontal axis (quantity demanded), but there's no requirement that it must be done this way. We could read from quantity to price. Consider Adam's marginal benefit curve for apples as shown in the following Figure 3-1.

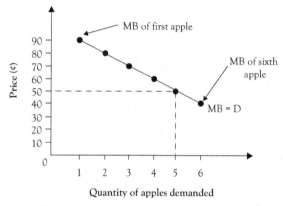

Figure 3-1. Adam's marginal benefit curve for apples.

We ask Adam how much the first apple is worth to him—perhaps in an auction context—and we are told 90¢. It is worth this much because he is willing to pay 90¢ to get it. Given the law of diminishing marginal utility, we would expect that the second apple would be worth less to Adam—perhaps only 80¢ and so on. Each apple's marginal benefit can be recorded as shown on the diagram and a marginal benefit curve plotted. But surely this is the demand curve! A demand curve plots the relationship between price and quantity demanded and we can see that, if the price of apples is 50¢, then Adam will wish to buy five apples. The demand curve and the marginal benefit curve are identical.

Consumer Surplus

Figure 3-1 contains other information of interest. **Consumer surplus** (or net consumer benefit) is the difference between the price that the buyer is willing to pay and the price he or she does pay. If the price of apples is 50¢, then Adam will buy the first apple (which he values at 90¢) for 40¢, a consumer surplus of 40¢ on that apple. The second apple will yield a consumer surplus of 30¢, and so on. Overall, Adam's consumer surplus from the five apples he buys is $1.00 (40¢ + 30¢ + 20¢ + 10¢ + 0¢). When he decides whether or not to buy each successive apple, Adam compares the marginal benefit received versus the price paid. He will buy if the marginal benefit exceeds the price. He will not buy the sixth apple because he would be giving up 50¢ in order to receive something worth only 40¢.

Graphically, the consumer surplus for each apple is the vertical distance between the marginal benefit curve and the price. It is the triangular area below the demand curve and above the price. Given the demand, a price reduction increases consumer surplus while a price increase reduces it.

THINK IT THROUGH: When you enter a car dealership you start an economic game. The salesperson tries to discover how high a price you are willing to pay—and you try not to tell him. The lower you can move the price, the greater your consumer surplus. The higher he can raise the price, without losing the sale, the more of your consumer surplus he can extract from you. Similarly, if the apple vendor could determine Adam's marginal benefit for each apple and then charge that price for each apple separately, then he could appropriate all of Adam's consumer surplus.

THINK IT THROUGH: The demand curve depicts marginal benefit. Review the factors that can shift the demand curve. Can you "translate" them into factors that can affect marginal benefit.

To maximize his consumer surplus, Adam should buy apples until the marginal benefit of the last apple bought (MB_A) equals the price (P_A). Thus

$$MB_A = P_A$$

Put differently

$$MB_A/P_A = 1$$

Across all goods the condition that will maximize Adam's consumer surplus is

$$MB_A/P_A = MB_B/P_B = MB_C/P_C \ldots = 1$$

This rather intimidating formula is identical in structure and operation to the utility maximization rule we developed earlier. All it is saying is that, in order to maximize consumer surplus, the buyer should purchase each good in amounts such that the marginal benefit per dollar is equal for all goods.

Do we follow this rule? No—this is a counsel of perfection and our real-world decisions are imperfect—but we should get as close to it as possible.

All maximizing consumers of apples should follow this rule, so, summing the benefits, we get the rule for maximizing total consumer surplus (total net consumer benefit):

$$\Sigma MB_A = P_A$$

where Σ means "the sum of."

We have assumed that Adam has sufficient income to buy every good up to the maximum amount that he wishes. This is unlikely! Given limited spending power, marginal benefit will exceed price, so

$$MB_A > P_A$$

The constrained maximization rule for all goods is

$$MB_A/P_A = MB_B/P_B = MB_C/P_C \ldots \geq 1$$

Review: In this section we have explored three related explanations for the negative slope of the demand curve. Two (marginal utility and marginal benefit) of the three are closely tied to the law of diminishing marginal utility, while the third (the substitution effect and the income effect) offer a somewhat different perspective.

Supply Revisited: Marginal Cost and Producer Surplus

In the previous section we discovered that marginal benefit is identical to demand and that consumer surplus is the difference between the maximum price a consumer is willing to pay and the market price. In this section we reach quite parallel conclusions on the supply side of the market.

Marginal Cost

We first came across marginal cost (MC) in Chapter 1, where we defined it as "the additional cost incurred when an additional unit of a good is produced." Fundamentally, marginal cost is opportunity cost, but it is also related to the supply curve.

A supply curve shows the relationship between price and quantity supplied. As we did with demand, let us read it from the horizontal axis (quantity supplied) to the vertical axis (price). Consider Eve's marginal cost curve for apples as shown in Figure 3-2.

We ask Eve what is the lowest price she will accept for the first apple she supplies and we are told 10¢. As this is the lowest price she will accept and still be willing to produce, this price must equal the cost of

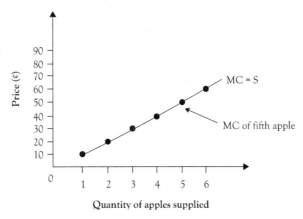

Figure 3-2. Eve's marginal cost curve for apples.

producing the apple—in other words, 10¢ is the marginal cost of the first apple.

Comment: There is a technical issue here regarding fixed cost, but, because it does not affect our general argument, we postpone a discussion of this point until Chapter 5.

Recall that in Chapter 1 we saw that production is subject to the law of increasing costs. Given this, we would expect that the second apple would cost more for Eve to produce—perhaps 20¢. And so on. Each apple's marginal cost can be recorded as shown on the diagram and a marginal cost curve plotted. It is the same as the supply curve! A supply curve plots the relationship between price and quantity supplied, and we can see that, if the price of apples is 50¢, then Eve will wish to sell five apples. The supply curve and the marginal cost curve are one and the same.

Producer Surplus

As with demand, our supply-side analysis has more to tell. **Producer surplus** (net producer benefit) is the difference between the lowest price that the seller is willing to accept for an item and the price he or she does receive. If the price of apples is 50¢, then Eve will sell the first apple—her producer surplus is 40¢. The second apple produced will yield Eve a producer surplus of 30¢, and so on. Eve's total producer surplus from the five apples she sells is $1.00 (40¢ + 30¢ + 20¢ + 10¢ + 0¢). When making the decision whether or not to produce each successive apple, Eve compares the revenue received and the marginal cost incurred. If the price exceeds the marginal cost, she will produce. She will not produce the sixth apple because the price would not cover the marginal cost of production.

To maximize her producer surplus, Eve should produce until the marginal cost of her product (MC_A) equals its price (P_A). Thus

$$MC_A = P_A$$

Put differently

$$MC_A/P_A = 1$$

All maximizing producers of apples should follow this rule, so, summing the costs, we get the rule for maximizing total producer surplus (total net producer benefit):

$$\Sigma MC_A = P_A$$

The condition that will maximize producer surplus for firms across all products is

$$MC_A/P_A = MC_B/P_B = MC_C/P_C \ldots = 1$$

Graphically, the producer surplus for each apple is the vertical distance between the marginal cost curve and the price. It is the triangular area above the supply curve and below the price. If price increases, then producer surplus increases too.

Maximizing Society's Total Economic Surplus

Consider Figure 3-3, which shows the market for apples. The market demand curve represents the sum of the marginal benefits received all buyers (ΣMB) and the market supply curve represents the sum of the marginal costs incurred by all sellers (ΣMC).

Figures depicting consumer and producer surplus conventionally have the demand and supply curves beginning at the vertical axis. Point X represents the maximum value that anyone would be willing to pay for an item whereas Point Y represents the lowest price at which any output

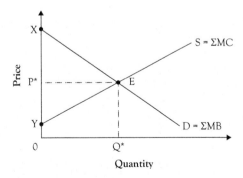

Figure 3-3. The market and efficiency.

will be offered for sale. P* and Q* are the equilibrium price and quantity respectively. The area P*XE represents the consumer surplus or total net benefit received by apple buyers whereas the area P*YE depicts the producer surplus or total net benefit received by apple sellers.

The area XYE represents the **total economic surplus**, or **total net benefit**, received by all market participants. This area—the overall net gain to members of society from the exchange of apples—is maximized when the market is at its equilibrium price and quantity. The area 0XEQ* represents the total benefit received by the recipients of Q* units while the area 0YEQ* represents the costs incurred in producing Q* units—the difference is the net gain.

If output is established at any level other than Q* then the total net benefit will be reduced. Consider Figure 3-4.

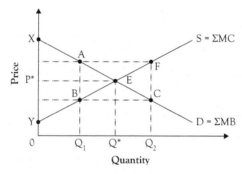

Figure 3-4. The market and an inefficient situation.

If producers limit output to Q_1 units then, for the last item exchanged, the marginal benefit exceeds the marginal cost. Any unit where the marginal benefit exceeds the marginal cost should be produced because there is a gain to society. All units up to Q* should be produced. By restricting output to Q_1, the market is forfeiting those additional gains and causing a **deadweight loss**. The benefit of the additional units is the area Q_1AEQ* while the cost of the additional units is the area Q_1BEQ*. The deadweight loss—the surplus given up—is the area BAE.

If, alternatively, producers expand output beyond Q* there is also a deadweight loss. At Q_2, for example, for the last item exchanged, the marginal benefit is less than the marginal cost. Such a unit should not be produced because there is a loss to society. Only units up to Q^* should be produced. By expanding output to Q_2, the market is reducing its total economic surplus. The benefit of the additional units beyond Q^* is the area Q^*ECQ_2, but the additional cost is the area Q^*EFQ_2. The deadweight loss in this case is the area CFE.

This point is quite subtle and central to microeconomics and therefore deserves comment. Recall that marginal cost is opportunity cost and that opportunity cost, in turn, is "the value of the next most preferred alternative given up" when a choice is made. If we choose to produce an apple and use resources to produce it, then the opportunity cost of that apple is the value we place on the items we otherwise would have produced with those resources. We make an allocatively efficient choice if the value gained by producing the apple exceeds the value given up, but, if the value gained is less than the value given up, then the choice is allocatively inefficient and shouldn't take place.

Summary: To maximize consumer surplus, buyers should buy until marginal benefit (MB) equals price (P) whereas, to maximize producer surplus, sellers should produce until marginal cost (MC) equals price. Thus

$$MB = P = MC$$

To maximize total economic surplus and achieve allocative efficiency, the market should produce the quantity at which marginal benefit equals marginal cost

$$MB = MC$$

If MB > MC, then production should increase; if MB < MC, then production should decrease.

Market Intervention: Price Ceilings and Price Floors

In the preceding section we established that markets that are allowed to achieve equilibrium maximize society's total economic surplus. This happy result is due to the activities of each individual participant pursuing his or her own self-interest within a free market. Adam Smith referred to this process as the "invisible hand" that directs market-driven economies to the allocatively efficient mix of goods and services.

Sometimes, however, governments feel the need to regulate markets. Two such forms of regulation are price ceilings and price floors.

Price Ceiling

A **price ceiling** is a maximum price limit imposed on a market. A price ceiling may be established at any price level, but an effective price ceiling is set *below* the equilibrium price and it causes a shortage in the market. The classic example of a price ceiling is the rent controls in New York and other cities.

THINK IT THROUGH: Can you think of other examples of restrictions that prevent price from rising above a set level? Usury laws set maximum interest rates that can be charged to borrowers. Price controls are frequent during wars or times of crisis. In 1973, in the face of rising prices for crude oil, the U.S. government limited the price of gasoline at the pumps. In 1979, northern states imposed a limit on home heating oil and California imposed controls on the wholesale electricity market in 2001.

THINK IT THROUGH: What happens if a price ceiling is set above the equilibrium price? Nothing happens! A price ceiling above the equilibrium price is nonbinding. Any supplier seeking to charge such a price would be left with unsold output and be forced to cut price to get rid of the surplus.

Price ceilings are not imposed malevolently—indeed usually they are well intentioned—but they have unintended adverse consequences. Figure 3-5 depicts the market for gasoline. (From this point on, we'll drop the "S" notation for marginal benefit and marginal cost.)

Let us suppose that a crisis in the Middle East has led to a disruption of oil supplies, reducing supply and driving up the price of gasoline. The market price of a gallon of gasoline is $7.00. We have established that a freely operating market will adjust to reach the allocatively efficient output level—the one that maximizes total economic surplus. However, a price of $7.00 per gallon will certainly cause severe hardship to many

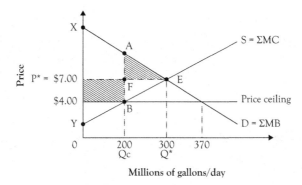

Figure 3-5. A price ceiling in the market for gasoline.

citizens, particularly the working poor who must travel to work and who will find it difficult to curtail their gasoline consumption.

The president intervenes and imposes a maximum price of $4.00 per gallon. (Here is the good intention!) The immediate effect of the price control is that there will be a gas shortage. In the absence of prices, some other method of rationing must emerge. The simplest method is "first come, first served," which will create lines at the gas pumps.

Graphical Analysis: The equilibrium market price (P*) is $7.00. At this price, the consumer surplus is P*XE, the producer surplus is P*YE, and the total economic surplus is YXE.

The price ceiling (P_c) is $4.00, the quantity supplied is 200 million gallons, the quantity demanded is 370 million gallons, and there is a shortage of 170 million gallons. Although consumers wish for more, only 200 million gallons are available. At P_c, the consumer surplus is P_cXAB (the difference between the demand curve and the price for the 200 million gallons that consumers can buy), the producer surplus is P_cYB, and the total economic surplus is YXAB.

The price ceiling has reduced the total economic surplus (by the deadweight loss BAE) and reapportioned the remainder of the economic surplus, with consumers gaining P_cP*FB but losing FAE, and producers losing P_cP*EB. Although some groups may gain, on balance, society loses because of the price ceiling.

Unintended effects of a price ceiling: The shortage will impose additional nonmarket costs on consumers. With a "first come, first served" rationing method, there will be additional search time to find sellers with gas to sell, queuing (and possible violence), and the risk of being stranded on the highway. Unscrupulous sellers may attempt to take advantage of the situation by requiring additional purchases before gas is pumped—a car wash, for example. Black markets may develop or the quality of gasoline (or the service provided) may be degraded, perhaps by the addition of cheaper additives. This is, after all, a seller's market.

THINK IT THROUGH: To alleviate some of these adverse effects, the government could ration gas by issuing coupons entitling drivers to a set amount of gasoline per month. How should these be allocated? Should it be equal shares for all? Is such a system "fair"? Note that, unless coupons are nontransferable, a market for *coupons* will develop with the more affluent members of society being able to buy and the less affluent losing out— precisely the result the price control was intended to prevent. If coupons are nontransferable, then the recipient has an incentive to buy gasoline, possibly to resell it.

Price Floor

A **price floor** is a minimum price limit imposed on a market. A price floor may be established at any price level, but an effective price floor is set *above* the equilibrium price and it causes a surplus. The classic example of a price floor is the minimum wage, although there have been price supports in agriculture, trucking, and the airline industry.

THINK IT THROUGH: What happens if a price floor is set below the equilibrium price? Nothing happens! A price floor set below equilibrium is nonbinding because, at a low price, the resulting shortages would push up the price until equilibrium was reestablished. A price floor does not prevent the price from rising.

Consider Figure 3-6. The equilibrium hourly wage is $6.00. However, politicians believe that a reasonable "living wage" is not less than $9.00 per hour and impose a minimum wage at that rate. The immediate effect of the wage control is that there will be a labor surplus where previously none existed.

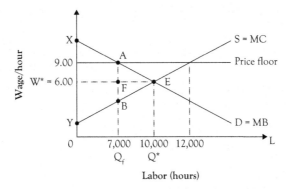

Figure 3-6. A price floor in the labor market.

Graphical Analysis: The demand curve is the demand for labor by employers and the supply curve is the supply of labor by workers seeking jobs. The equilibrium market wage (W*) is $6.00. At this wage, the consumer surplus is W*XE, the producer surplus is W*YE, and the total economic surplus is YXE.

The price floor (W$_f$) is $9.00, the quantity of labor supplied is 12,000 hours, the quantity demanded is 7,000 hours, and there is a surplus of 5,000 hours. Although workers wish for more job opportunities, only 7,000 hours at the increased wage rate. At W$_f$, the consumer surplus is W$_f$XA (the difference between the demand curve and the price for the 7,000 hours that employers will hire), the producer surplus for workers is W$_f$YBA, and the total economic surplus is YXAB.

The minimum wage has reduced the total economic surplus (by the deadweight loss BAE) and reapportioned the remainder of the surplus, with workers gaining W$_f$W*FA but losing FBE, and employers losing W$_f$W*EA. As with a price ceiling, some groups may gain, but, on balance, society loses because of the minimum wage. Note that, whereas at equilibrium, there was a job for all interested workers, the imposition of the wage floor creates unemployment, partly through an increase in workers seeking jobs and partly through a reduction in job opportunities.

The bottom line is that even well-intentioned efforts to prevent markets from reaching equilibrium threaten the efficiency of the economic system. Unless there is a very strong reason otherwise, our goal ought to be to foster competitive equilibrium in all markets.

Further Applications: Rent Controls, Butter Mountains and Milk Lakes, Scalping, and Gift-Giving

We can find many other examples of the inefficiencies wreaked by well-intentioned government intervention into free markets. The effects of a price ceiling or a price floor have already been outlined—the graphical analysis is generally applicable—but the particulars will vary from context to context. Some additional examples follow.

Rent Controls

Among the most well-reported price ceiling are the rent control regulations in New York and other cities. Rent control was introduced as a "temporary" wartime measure in 1943 to alleviate hardships for the families of soldiers as rents and other prices rose. The argument was still being made in 2005 when Mayor Bloomberg stated that "poor people who were here during the hard times shouldn't be priced out." However, respected economist Assar Lindbeck noted that "next to bombing, rent control seems in many cases to be the most efficient technique so far known for destroying cities."

The situation is presented in Figure 3-7.

In the absence of rent control, the market price of a two-bedroom, two-bathroom is P* and the allocatively efficient number of apartments is Q*. However, this price imposes severe hardship on many renters, particularly the poor. Rent control imposes a maximum rent for such

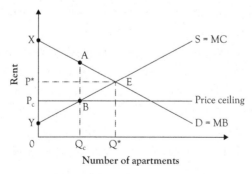

Figure 3-7. Rent control.

an apartment at P_c. Immediately, the quantity of apartments demanded increases to Q_d and quantity supplied decreases to Q_c, causing a shortage of Q_cQ_d.

Graphical Analysis: The equilibrium market rent is P*. Given this rent, the consumer surplus for renters is P*XE, the producer surplus is P*YE, and the total economic surplus is YXE.

The controlled rent is P_c, the quantity supplied is Q_c, the quantity demanded is Q_d. At P_c, the consumer surplus for tenants is P_cXAB, the producer surplus for landlords is P_cYB, and the total economic surplus is YXAB.

Rent control reduces the total economic surplus (by the deadweight loss BAE) and divides the remaining of the economic surplus, with consumers gaining P_cP*FB but losing FAE, and producers losing P_cP*EB. Renters with apartments probably gain but, on balance, society loses because of rent control.

Unintended effects of rent control:

Some method must be found to allocate the available apartments. It is a seller's market and we might expect discrimination—ethnic, sexual or racial, or against families with children or pets, or with an unreliable financial history. Bribes, key money, nonrefundable deposits to cover potential damage, or an "agreement" to pay over the odds could occur.

Meanwhile, with so many potential renters, landlords may not need to maintain properties in good trim to attract tenants, causing apartments to fall into disrepair or harbor vermin, lowering property values throughout the neighborhood. Also, there may be an incentive for current renters to stay in their rent-controlled apartments. A family (husband, wife, several children) may have occupied a large apartment at a low rent. As the children move out, it would make sense to down-size but, if this means moving into accommodation that is not rent-controlled, then the family may decide to stay on in the large apartment. Self-interest in the face of market controls leads to a misallocation of apartments.

As time goes by, the shortage may intensify as the quantity of rental properties supplied may be further reduced as apartments become dilapidated or are converted into condos, offices, or some other form of structure that is not covered by rent control.

Butter Mountains and Milk Lakes

Since its earliest days, a fundamental plank in the structure of the Common Market (the organization that has evolved into the European Union) has been its Common Agricultural Policy (CAP). This complex mixture of subsidies, price supports, and other measures was intended to ensure sufficiently high prices for high-cost and inefficient small farmers and, among other elements, price floors were imposed. The fear was that liberalized competition and trade would bankrupt small farmers in particular regions; the intention was to prevent this from happening. The result was predictable—surplus output such as the infamous butter mountains and wine lakes.

Consider the operation of a price support in the market for milk as shown in Figure 3-8. The equilibrium price for milk is P* and the equilibrium quantity is Q*. At this price, the consumer surplus is P*XE, the producer surplus for dairy farmers is P*YE, and the total economic surplus is YXE.

Administrators in Brussels tell farmers that the minimum price is guaranteed to be P_f and that any surplus output will be bought by the government. If a price floor (P_f) is imposed, then the quantity supplied of milk is Q_s, the quantity demanded is Q_f and a surplus of Q_fQ_s liters

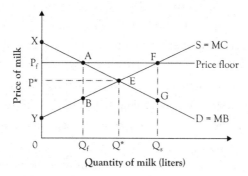

Figure 3-8. An agricultural price support.

results. At P_f, the consumer surplus is P_fXA (the difference between the demand curve and the price for the amount of milk that will be bought by consumers). Because the government stands ready to buy any surplus milk, the producer surplus for farmers from sales to consumers is P_fYBA.

Now consider the area Q_fAFQ_s. This represents the payment to farmers by the government for the surplus milk. The producer surplus for this milk is BAF. However, if the government resells the milk to the highest bidders, society's valuation of this milk is only Q_fAGQ_s and the loss to the government (taxpayers)—AFG—must be set against the gain to farmers. Overall, the deadweight loss in total economic surplus is FGE.

THINK IT THROUGH: At Q_s, there is an inefficient overproduction of milk—marginal benefit is less than marginal cost. The marginal cost of the extra milk is Q*EFQ_s whereas the marginal benefit is only Q*EGQ_s. The difference represents the deadweight loss.

Unintended effects of guaranteed agricultural price supports:

The price support benefits dairy farmers at the expense of consumers and taxpayers. The CAP is a long-running grievance in member countries with small agricultural sectors, such as Britain whose politicians have argued that it is a form of income redistribution within the Union.

We have assumed that the surplus milk is sold to the highest bidder, but, in practice, this may not be feasible as reselling of the cheaper milk would result in a black market. Milk that is not sold by the government must be stored, but such "milk lakes" involve additional resources and costs.

Other options include destroying the milk, converting the milk into butter and cheese, donating surpluses as aid to developing countries or subsidizing farmers to export at artificially low prices.

Scalping

One consequence of holding prices artificially low is that black markets appear. Anyone attending a popular concert or sports event has seen scalpers. Although scalpers have a bad name, they fulfill a valuable economic function by bringing together those with the greatest wish to buy a ticket and the ticket they desire. In fact, there's no significant difference between the activity of the scalper and any other type of voluntary exchange—he wants your money and you want his ticket. Both participants gain if the price is mutually acceptable.

Gift-giving and Inefficiency

After each holiday season, we witness the queues of shoppers returning unwanted gifts. All this activity indicates an inefficiency in the gift-giving process. The highly-priced Justin Beiber t-shirt bought for me by my granddaughter,   although kindly meant, does not suit my post-hippie style. The amount that she spent (the marginal cost) is greater than the value that I receive (the marginal benefit) and the number of Justin Beiber t-shirts should be reduced. In fact, gifts in kind or gift cards are less efficient as gifts than hard cash. With a gift card, you are restricted in your choices. With a gift in kind, you receive the gift the donor wishes you to have (whether you like it or not); with an equivalent amount of cash, you can receive the gift *you* wish you to have or, if it is preferable to a gift, you can save!

CHAPTER 4

Elasticity

By the end of this chapter you will be able to:

1. Describe and apply the concept of elasticity.
2. Interpret the terms elastic, inelastic, and unit elastic as related to price elasticity of demand.
3. Use the intuitive "percentage change" formula and the midpoint formula to measure price elasticity of demand.
4. Apply the total revenue test to predict the effect on total revenue of a price change, given different price elasticity circumstances.
5. List and explain the effects of the determinants of price elasticity of demand.
6. Calculate and interpret income elasticity of demand and cross-price elasticity of demand using the intuitive "percentage change" formula.
7. Calculate and interpret elasticity values for the price elasticity of supply.

Have you ever shopped around for the best price on airline tickets or hotel accommodation? Most of us have and, nowadays, the Internet helps us to do this with sites such as Travelocity and Expedia. But have you ever shopped around for the best price on electricity service for your home? Probably not, because, for most of us, the electricity company we have is a "take it or leave it" situation and we have little flexibility short of installing our own solar panels. In the case of airline tickets, we can be choosy and responsive to price differences, but in the case of electricity, we can't. This brings us to a consideration of "elasticity."

Chapter Preview: In this chapter we consider ways of quantifying some of the relationships we discussed qualitatively in Chapter 2. In a way, this entire chapter may be seen as a series of applications of concepts that you have already learned.

Elasticity—A Measure of Responsiveness

The Big Idea of Elasticity

Students of economics frequently complain that, although there is lots of theory, there are few practical numbers based on real-world experience. We know, for example, that an increase in price causes a decrease in quantity demanded but we don't know *how much* of a decrease there is. Is it a big decrease or a small decrease? **Elasticity** (a fancy word for "responsiveness" or "sensitivity") answers this sort of a question. *Price elasticity of demand* measures how responsive or sensitive demanders are to a change in price—how much they react to a price change? *Income elasticity of demand* measures how much demanders respond when income level changes—if there is a recession and income levels fall, how much will the demand for cars decrease? *Cross-price elasticity of demand* measures how much the demand for one good changes when the price of a related good changes—if the price of Coca-Cola increases, how much does the demand for Pepsi increase? *Price elasticity of supply* measures how much the quantity supplied of a good will increase as its price rises—is it a large response (relatively "elastic") or a small response (relatively "inelastic")?

In any elasticity calculation, we measure the extent of the change in one variable relative to the change in another variable. We could, for example, develop an "advertising elasticity of demand" to show how much the demand for our product changes as our advertising budget increases.

Price Elasticity of Demand

Considering price elasticity of demand, we can establish an "intuitive" formula that will answer many of our questions quite simply. Price elasticity of demand (E_d) measures how much quantity demanded (Q_d) changes as price (P) changes. Our intuitive formula would look like this:

E_d = percentage change in quantity demanded/percentage change in price.

We can make this look a bit more mathematical by translating it in the following way:

$$E_d = \%\Delta\, Q_d \,/\, \%\Delta P$$

where "Δ" is the mathematical symbol (delta) for "change in."

Comment: Note that the "dollars" term is in the denominator and the "numbers" term is in the numerator. This is the typical elasticity pattern and we'll see it repeated in each elasticity formula in this chapter— numbers on top and dollars on the bottom.

To see how this formula works, think of a good like gasoline. Suppose that the price of gas jumps by ten percent. (At the time of writing, a gallon of gas costs about \$3.75, so we're talking about a price hike of almost 40¢ to about a price of \$4.10.) We know quantity demanded will decrease, but probably it will not decrease by much. After all, most of us buy what we need and it's difficult and inconvenient to change our habits. Let's say quantity demanded may fall by two percent. Using the intuitive formula:

$$E_d = \%\Delta\, Q_d / \%\Delta P = -2/+10 = -0.2.$$

In absolute values, E_d is 0.2.

Price Elasticity of Demand—An Absolute Value?

Because negative values are difficult to work with and because we know from the Law of Demand that there is a negative relationship between price and quantity demanded, from now on we'll use the absolute value for price elasticity of demand. In this example, then, $E_d = 0.2$.

An elasticity value ("coefficient") of 0.2 indicates that demand is not very responsive to a price change. We know that demand is relatively inelastic because, although price has risen by ten percent, drivers are still buying almost the same amount of gas at the pumps. The lower the elasticity coefficient the less responsive (less elastic) demand is.

Now consider a product such as Coca-Cola. Suppose the price of Coke increases by ten percent. Although some buyers will continue to favor Coke, many will switch to alternatives such as Pepsi or Dr. Pepper.

There will be a vigorous (elastic) response. One study reported a price elasticity value of 3.8 for Coca-Cola. To interpret this number, go back to the intuitive formula.

$$E_d = \%\Delta\, Q_d\, /\, \%\Delta P = \%\Delta\, Q_d\, /\, +10 = 3.8$$

So the percentage change in quantity demanded is thirty-eight percent. We conclude that a ten percent increase in the price of Coke will result in a thirty-eight percent decline in the quantity demanded of Coke.

Lower elasticity numbers are relatively inelastic and higher elasticity numbers are relatively elastic. A coefficient of zero would tell us that buyers are completely unresponsive to changes in price (perfectly inelastic demand) whereas the more extremely sensitive buyers are to even tiny price changes, then the closer the elasticity value approaches its maximum value of infinity. The boundary between "inelastic" and "elastic" demand, where demand is unit-elastic demand, has an elasticity coefficient of 1.0. A ten percent increase in price will cause a ten percent decrease in quantity demanded.

The following line diagram (Figure 4-1) summarizes what we have learned so far about price elasticity of demand.

Challenge: Use the intuitive formula to verify that zero is the coefficient when demand is perfectly inelastic and that infinity is the coefficient when demand is perfectly elastic.

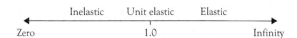

Figure 4-1. Price elasticity of demand.

As shown in Figure 4-2, the perfectly inelastic demand curve graphs as a vertical line and the perfectly elastic demand curve graphs as a horizontal line.

Total Revenue Test

The Total Revenue Test is a convenient way to determine a good's elasticity within a given price range. **Total Revenue** (TR) or total spending is defined as price (P) multiplied by quantity demanded (Q).

$$TR = P \times Q$$

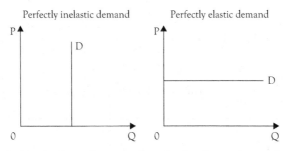

Figure 4-2. Perfectly inelastic and perfectly elastic demand curves.

First, consider gasoline. The demand for gas is inelastic ($E_d < 1.0$), because we have very little ability to buy less when the price increases. What would happen to the number of dollars you'd have to spend on gas if the price rose? Would you spend more dollars, or fewer? If you resemble most buyers, then you'd spend more money at the pumps. We can conclude that, for a good with an inelastic demand, if price increases, then total revenue will increase. Similarly, if price decreases then, if we have a good with an inelastic demand, total spending on that good would decrease.

Consider Coca-Cola, however. Coke, we know is a good with an elastic demand ($E_d > 1.0$). If the price of Coke increases, many buyers will switch to other alternatives, such as Pepsi or Sprite. The total number of dollars spent on Coke will decrease. For a good with an elastic demand, if price increases, then total revenue will decrease. Similarly, if we have a good with an elastic demand, then total spending on that good would increase when price decreases.

For a good with a unit elastic demand ($E_d = 1.0$), total revenue does not change as price increases or decreases.

Total Revenue Test Summary:
As price increases, demand is inelastic if total revenue increases.
As price increases, demand is elastic if total revenue decreases.
As price increases, demand is unit elastic if total revenue is unaffected.

Slope ≠ Elasticity: From what has been said so far, and from the previous figures, it would be tempting to infer that, the steeper the demand curve, the smaller the price elasticity of demand, but this is incorrect.

Consider the following demand schedule for apples and its associated demand curve (Table 4-1).

Table 4-1. Demand and Total Revenue

Price	Quantity Demanded	Total Revenue
S6	2	$12
S5	4	$20
S4	6	$24
$3	8	$24
$2	10	$20
$1	12	$12

Note that, as price rises from $5 to $6, total revenue decreases from $20 to $12. Using the total revenue test, the decrease in total revenue as a consequence of the price increase is enough to tell us that demand is elastic in that price range.

Challenge: Use the total revenue test to classify elasticity in the price ranges $4 to $5, $3 to $4, $2 to $3, and $1 to $2. (It should be elastic, unit elastic, inelastic, and inelastic, respectively.) In each of the examples, price increased. Does it make any difference to your results if, instead, price decreases? It doesn't!

The demand curve in Figure 4-3 graphs as a straight line—its slope is constant—but the elasticity is not constant. Using the total revenue test, we can see that, at high prices, demand is elastic whereas, at low prices, demand is inelastic and that there is an inelastic area in the middle of the range. Accordingly, although elasticity certainly is related to the slope of the demand curve, it is distinct from it.

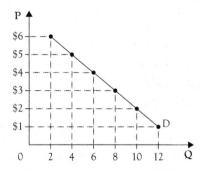

Figure 4-3. Slope ≠ elasticity.

The Midpoint Formula

The total revenue test allows us to categorize elasticity in a price range as "elastic," "inelastic," or "unit elastic," but it does not provide precise elasticity values. The "intuitive" formula that we've already seen can be used if the percentage changes in price and quantity are known but, if only the prices and quantities are known, then the best approach is to use the "midpoint" formula.

Given that price changes from P_1 to P_2, the intent behind the midpoint formula is to derive the average of the initial price (P_1) and the final price (P_2) to get ($P_2 + P_1$)/2 and, similarly, to derive the average of the initial quantity (Q_1) and the final quantity (Q_2) to get ($Q_2 + Q_1$)/2. The change in price is ($P_2 - P_1$) while the change in quantity is ($Q_2 - Q_1$). To interpret: The formula is comparing the change in quantity ($Q_2 - Q_1$) to an "average" or midpoint quantity, ($Q_2 + Q_1$)/2 and, similarly, comparing the change in price ($P_2 - P_1$) to an "average" or midpoint price, ($P_2 + P_1$)/2.

By canceling the 2s in the formula, it can be simplified (a little!) to:

$$\frac{(Q_2 - Q_1)/(Q_2 + Q_1)}{(P_2 - P_1)/(P_2 + P_1)}$$

Simplified, but still quite intimidating! Let us return to Table 4-1 and determine the elasticity coefficient between $5 and $6. From the total revenue test, we know that we should expect to get a coefficient that is greater than 1.0 (elastic). Let P_1 be $5; P_2 be $6; Q_1 be 4; and Q_2 be 2. Plug the values into the midpoint formula.

$$E_d = [(2 - 4)/(2 + 4)]/[(\$6 - \$5)/(\$6 + \$5)] = 3.67 \text{ (in absolute terms)}$$

Challenge: Calculate the elasticity coefficients in each of the following price ranges—$4 to $5, $3 to $4, $2 to $3, and $1 to $2. (Your results should be 1.80, 1.00, 0.56, and 0.27, respectively, in absolute terms.)

Review: What do the numbers mean again? The elasticity number tells us how much quantity demanded changes in response to a change in price. Use the intuitive formula to interpret the coefficients. Given that $E_d = 3.67$, we could state that "If there is a 10 percent increase in the price of this good, then we'd expect to see a 36.7 percent decrease in quantity demanded and, because this coefficient shows an elastic demand, the price increase would cause total revenue to decrease."

Learning Tip: If all you need is to determine whether demand is "elastic" or "inelastic," then the total revenue test is sufficient. Use the midpoint formula only if you require a numerical result.

Determinants of Price Elasticity of Demand

What factors influence our ability or willingness to respond when the price of a good changes? Responsiveness can be affected by the availability of substitutes, the importance of the item in the buyer's overall budget, whether the good is perceived as a necessity, the length of time involved in adjusting to the price change, and whether the user of the good is also the buyer of the good.

Availability of substitutes: The greater the number of close substitutes the easier it is to switch from one product to another. Frequently, companies will advertise to increase brand loyalty or will offer incentives to returning customers in order to blunt sensitivity to price differences between their own and other products. Store- or product-specific credit cards or coupons, frequent buyer discount cards, and preferential treatment are designed to increase loyalty and to reduce the impulse to shop around.

The broader the definition of a product, the less elastic the demand for it. While the price elasticity of demand for Miller beer may be quite high, the price elasticity of demand for beer in general is less so.

THINK IT THROUGH: Can you see that advertising frequently is intended to differentiate between "our" product and the competitors' products in order to reduce price elasticity?

Importance of the item in the buyer's overall budget: The more significant an item is in one's overall budget, the more likely it is that a price change will have an impact on the buyer's behavior. The less important an item is, the less likely it is that buyers will be sensitive to a price change. Evidence to support this view includes studies showing that teenage cigarette smokers, while having an inelastic demand for cigarettes, have a *less* inelastic demand than that of their more affluent parents.

THINK IT THROUGH: By this argument, which should have the greater (more elastic) demand, gasoline or bottled water? If the price of table salt doubled, how much would most consumers care?

Necessity or luxury: By definition, a necessity is something that the buyer cannot do without, even if the price increases, while a luxury is optional. Prescription medicines are likely to have low price elasticities, while elective "vanity" surgeries may not.

Length of time to adjust to the price change: It may be quite difficult to find satisfactory substitutes for the good whose price has increased in the period immediately following the price increase. As time goes by, though, more alternatives may become available. The longer the buyer has to shop around and adjust to a price change the more effective that adjustment will be. We would expect price elasticities to increase as time passes.

THINK IT THROUGH: Suppose that, tomorrow, the price of a gallon of gasoline doubled permanently. How effectively could you respond the next day or week? The next month? The next year? Most car owners would complain bitterly but, initially, would have to pay and suffer at the pump. We might trim back on some trips but, beyond that, it would be difficult to reduce fuel consumption. Car-pooling, public transport, or biking might be feasible alternatives but many consumers are reluctant to change their preferred behaviors and traditions. With the passage of time, we might buy a new more fuel-efficient car, or move closer to work, or adjust our schedule to work at home one day, and so on, but all these responses take time to implement.

Whether the user of the good is also the buyer of the good: Demand may be less price-sensitive if there is a disconnect between the person who uses a good and the person who pays for it.

THINK IT THROUGH: If you have an expense account, or will be reimbursed for a purchase, are you really as discriminating about purchases as you would be if it were your "own" money?

Income Elasticity of Demand

Income elasticity of demand (Y_d) looks at how much the demand (D) for a good changes as income level (Y) changes. From Chapter 2 we know that there are normal goods and inferior goods. With a *normal good*, if income increases, then the demand for the good will increase—there is a positive relationship between "percentage change in income" and "percentage change in demand" when we have a normal good. However, the income elasticity of demand coefficient will be negative for an *inferior good*—as income level increases, the demand for an inferior good will decrease. Our intuitive formula would look like this:

Y_d = percentage change in demand/percentage change in income.

More mathematically, this could be expressed the following way:

$Y_d = \%\Delta D / \%\Delta Y$

Comment: Note that the financial term is in the denominator and the "numbers" term is in the numerator, as we saw with price elasticity of demand and as we'll see again with the other elasticity formulas that follow. This is the typical "elasticity" pattern.

Figure 4-4 summarizes what we have learned so far about income elasticity of demand.

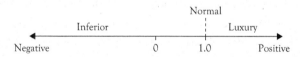

Figure 4-4. Income elasticity of demand.

The farther from zero (no response) we go, in either direction, the greater the buyers' response to a change in income. Goods whose income elasticity exceeds +1.0 are sometimes termed "luxury" or "supernormal" goods.

The income elasticity of demand for cars is very high (+2.46, according to one study). What does this value mean? First, because the number is positive, we know that this is a normal good. Choosing ten percent as a convenient value for the percentage change in income, we get

$$Y_d = \%\Delta D/ +10 = +2.46$$

Solving this, the percentage increase in the demand for cars would be 24.6 percent if income increased by ten percent. You can see why executives in the car industry would be concerned if there was a likelihood of recession!

The income elasticity of demand for public transport is negative (−0.36, according to a study). Because the number is negative, we know that this is an inferior good. Again choosing ten percent as a convenient value for the percentage change in income, we get

$$Y_d = \%\Delta D/ +10 = -0.36$$

Solving this, the percentage decrease in the demand for public transport would be 3.6 percent if income increased by ten percent. We would predict increased ridership on public transport during an economic slowdown.

Challenge: Many states have introduced lotteries. One argument against lotteries is that they act like a tax (albeit a voluntary one), and that poor citizens tend to be taxed more. In other words, lotteries are a form of regressive taxation. A study showed that the income elasticity of demand for lottery tickets was −0.7. Does this evidence lend support to the objection to lottery tickets?

Cross-Price Elasticity of Demand

Cross-price elasticity of demand (X_d) measures the degree by which the demand for one good changes when the price of a related good changes. In Chapter 2 we learned that if the price of Good B increases, then the demand for a substitute Good A will increase—there is a positive relationship between "percentage change in the price of Good B" and "percentage change in the demand for Good A" when the goods are substitutes. By contrast, the relationship will be negative in the case of complements. If goods are independent, the elasticity value will be zero.

Our intuitive formula would look like this:

X_{dAB} = percentage change in demand for Good A/percentage change in price of Good B.

This could be expressed the following way:

$X_{dAB} = \%\Delta D_{A} / \%\Delta P_{B}$

THINK IT THROUGH: We know that two goods that are substitutes have a positive cross-price elasticity. Coke and Pepsi are such goods but so are Coke and Sprite. However, Coke and Sprite are less close substitutes than are Coke and Pepsi. Will the cross-price elasticity coefficient between Coke and Sprite be higher than or lower than that between Coke and Pepsi? (The answer follows!)

Figure 4-5 summarizes what we have learned about cross-price elasticity of demand.

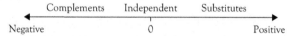

Figure 4-5. Cross-price elasticity of demand.

The cross-price elasticity relationship between Coke and Pepsi is estimated to be about +0.5. The positive sign confirms our belief that the two goods are substitutes. We would interpret the value as meaning that, if Coke hiked its price by ten percent, then the demand for Pepsi would increase by five percent. Coke and Sprite are substitutes but, because the relationship is weaker, the effect of Coke's price increase would lead to a comparatively weak increase in the demand for Sprite.

If rum and Coke are complements, then an increase in the price of Coke would lead to a decrease in the demand for rum. Bacardi would prefer Coca-Cola to keep its prices low and has an interest in U.S. agricultural policy's stance toward abundant corn production and low-price high fructose corn syrup.

THINK IT THROUGH: Suppose the cross-price elasticity relationship between Good A and Good B is E_{dAB} = +0.7. Would you expect the reverse relationship to have the same value? In other words, would E_{dBA} = +0.7?

Probably not. One of the goods may have many uses. For cooks, butter and margarine are substitutes but the impact on the demand for butter of an increase in the price of margarine is likely to be small. However, an increase in the price of butter may see many more cooks switching to margarine.

Price Elasticity of Supply

Price elasticity of supply (E_s) measures how much quantity supplied (Q_s) changes as price (P) changes. Our intuitive formula would look like this:

E_s = percentage change in quantity supplied/percentage change in price.

A more mathematical representation is

$E_s = \%\Delta Q_s / \%\Delta P$

The law of supply convinces us to expect that the price elasticity of supply values will be positive because an increase in the price of a good should cause an increase in its quantity supplied. If the price of gasoline increases, then we'd expect to see an increase in the production of gasoline. At one extreme, if a price increase caused no change in production then supply would be perfectly inelastic and the coefficient would be zero. At the other extreme, if a price increase provoked a very vigorous expansion in production then supply would be perfectly elastic and the coefficient would be infinitely large.

THINK IT THROUGH: Can the price elasticity of supply value be negative? What would this mean and why might it happen? What would the supply curve look like in such a case? (Answers follow.)

The interpretation of the elasticity coefficient for supply is quite similar to that of demand. Lower elasticity numbers are relatively inelastic and higher elasticity numbers are relatively elastic. A value that is less than one is inelastic, while a value greater than one is elastic. An elasticity coefficient of 0.2 indicates that supply is not very responsive to a price change but a coefficient of 2.4 shows that output is highly responsive.

One study reported a price elasticity of supply coefficient of 0.7 for oil production within the United States. To interpret this number, refer to the intuitive formula and assume that the price of oil has risen by ten percent. Substituting in values, we have

$$E_S = \%\Delta\, Q_S / \%\Delta P = \%\Delta\, Q_S\, / +10 = 0.7$$

therefore the percentage change in quantity supplied is seven percent. We conclude that a ten percent increase in the price of oil will result in a seven percent increase in the quantity supplied of oil by American producers.

Figure 4-6 summarizes what we have learned so far about price elasticity of supply.

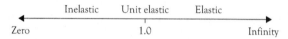

Figure 4-6. Price elasticity of supply.

There is no equivalent for price elasticity of supply of demand's total revenue test. We could derive a midpoint formula (the formula would be identical to that for demand) but we do not need it.

Determinants of Price Elasticity of Supply

What factors affect our ability or willingness to change production levels when the price of a good changes? For most goods, the major factor impacting responsiveness is the time available to adjust to the price change. Other factors, such as mobility or availability of resources, extent of excess production capacity, and the complexity of the production process in some sense also depend on time. An additional factor may be the convenience and cost of storage.

Length of time to adjust to the price change: The longer the producer has to adjust to a price change the more effective that adjustment can be. We would expect elasticity to increase as time passes and more alternatives become feasible. It may be quite costly (or perhaps impossible) to find, hire, and train additional resources for the good whose price has increased in the period immediately following a price increase. As time goes by, specialized resources and less costly options may become available.

We would expect elasticity to be greater in the aftermath of a recession, with machines and factories idle and many workers unemployed and highly motivated to work, than at the height of an economic boom. Also, goods with simple production processes, requiring little in the way of specialized resources, should be responsive more quickly than goods with highly specialized requirements, such as research and development facilities or expensive capital.

THINK IT THROUGH: With fewer steps and less complexity in the production process, will eggs sold locally have a greater elasticity of supply than store-bought "oven ready" chicken? What might reduce the ability of the local farmer to expand production quickly?

Convenience and cost of storage: These factors influence inventory holdings. Recall from Chapter 2 that supply refers to the willingness and ability to produce (*and make available for sale*) a quantity of a good or service. Markets are not concerned with production or the number of items stored in a warehouse but, rather, with the presence of that output where it can be sold. The supply of fireworks is concentrated around the Fourth of July, but stockpiling goes on for months before that time.

The producer's wish to hold inventory may depend on a desire to smooth production over time—as we've noted, spikes in production can be costly. But storage can be costly too. Perishable or bulky low-value items are likely to have a less elastic supply than stable or small items with a high value.

THINK IT THROUGH: Compare wheat and corn. Wheat is a "dry" grain, while corn contains more moisture and requires more careful storage. Which good has the greater price elasticity of supply? It is wheat.

The Short Run and the Long Run: Over 100 years ago, the British economist Alfred Marshall was spending a lot of his time thinking about time as it applies to economics. He had developed the concept of elasticity and realized that price elasticity of supply was strongly affected by the time frame involved. He defined two conceptual time periods—the short run and the long run.

The **short run** is defined as a period of time during which all but one of a firm's resources can be varied. In the short run, at least one resource is fixed in quantity. Because human resources can be hired or fired fairly readily the fixed resource is usually thought of as some sort of capital resource such as a nuclear reactor (electricity generation), an oil rig (oil production), a Mack truck (trucking industry), and so on. Clearly, though, the skills of a brain surgeon might be quite inflexible.

All resources are variable in the **long run**—any resource can be increased, decreased, or discarded. It is only in the long run that a firm can enter or leave an industry. In the short run, you may cut production, or even close your doors but, until you reach the long run, you still have the doors! Only when the firm has sold off all of its resources can it truly be said to have left the industry. Similarly, a firm seeking to enter an industry from scratch may be able to assemble some of its resources in the short run, but, because at least one resource is fixed at zero, it cannot be said to have entered the industry.

This is a conceptual distinction, not a calendar one. The time necessary to reach the long run will differ from industry to industry. A firm seeking to begin generating nuclear power faces a long road while an entrepreneur wishing to open a family restaurant will move through the process more rapidly.

Negative Price Elasticity of Supply—Is It Possible?: The law of supply suggests that the price elasticity of supply will be positive (higher price, so higher quantity supplied) but, in some rare instances, especially in the labor market, negative elasticities have been discovered.

THINK IT THROUGH: What can this mean for the appearance of the supply curve and when might it occur? A negative elasticity would imply that the supply curve is negatively sloped or "backward bending." This may occur at high income levels where the value of leisure time becomes more prized. Leisure is a normal good, so the demand for leisure increases as income increases until, eventually, the incentive to substitute work for leisure is overcome by the preference for leisure. With a salary increase, a rich lawyer or surgeon may decide to trim back on appointments or take early retirement and spend more time on the golf course.

THINK IT THROUGH: In Chapter 3 we discussed the substitution effect and the income effect as an explanation for the shape of the demand curve. Can you apply those concepts to explain the backward-bending labor supply curve? As the reward for labor increases, workers will substitute labor for leisure, working more intensively. Time-and-a-half, double time, or bonuses are offers intended to have this substitution effect. However, there is also an income effect if wage is increased. Because leisure is a normal good, the income effect of a wage increase is to reduce labor supply. If the income effect dominates the substitution effect, then the result is a backward-bending labor supply curve and a negative price elasticity of supply.

Applications

The Incidence of Taxes: Earlier in this chapter we concluded that the slope of a demand curve is not the same thing as its elasticity and as a general statement that is correct. However, if two demand curves with differing slopes intersect then we can say that the steeper demand curve is relatively less elastic than the other. We can use this result to analyze the incidence of taxes.

Let's suppose we have two states, West Carolina and East Carolina, that are similar in all respects except one—the residents of West Carolina are heavily addicted to locally produced whiskey while the residents of East Carolina are not.

We should expect to see the more inelastic (price-insensitive) demand for whiskey in West Carolina. The two demand curves are drawn in Figure 4-7, with West Carolina's demand labeled D_W and East Carolina's labeled D_E. Let us now suppose that the production of whiskey is the same in the two states and draw a single supply curve (S)—think of this as two supply curves, one on top of the other. In each state, the equilibrium price of whiskey is $6.00 per bottle and the equilibrium quantity is 10,000 bottles sold each week.

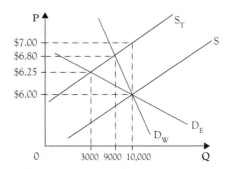

Figure 4-7. Incidence of a tax.

The governor of each state imposes a $1.00 tax on each bottle of whiskey produced. This tax will be collected from the sellers. This excise tax is similar to the "per gallon" tax imposed by many states on gasoline and the effect is best thought of as shifting the supply curve vertically upwards by the extent of the tax. The new supply curve is labeled S_T.

THINK IT THROUGH: Can you see why the supply curve will shift vertically by a dollar? A supply curve shows the relationship between the lowest price a supplier is willing to accept and the quantity supplied. If suppliers were willing to accept $6.00 per bottle before the tax in order to supply 10,000 bottles, then, after the introduction of the tax, the lowest price they'll be willing to accept to supply 10,000 bottles will be $7.00 per bottle.

As we'd expect, the imposition of the tax increases the price of whiskey. Note that it increases more in West Carolina because demand is relatively less elastic. The (nonaddicted) East Carolinians are more sensitive to price changes and, as price starts to increase, they will cut back in purchases.

Someone must pay the $1.00 tax on each bottle of whiskey purchased. Does elasticity affect who pays? We can see that the price in West Carolina has risen a great deal—most (80¢ per bottle) of the burden of the tax is being borne by consumers with only 20¢ per bottle being paid by producers. In East Carolina, by contrast, although some of the tax (25¢ per bottle) has been passed on to consumers, the bulk of the tax (the remaining 75¢ per bottle) is being paid by the producers.

We can conclude that the lower the price elasticity of demand the greater the fraction of the tax that can be passed on by producers to consumers.

Elasticity and Tax Revenues: We can take this story farther—which sort of good should a government seek to tax if it wishes to maximize its tax revenues? Goods that have an inelastic demand! In East Carolina, tax receipts will be $3,000 per day because only 3,000 bottles are being sold but, in West Carolina, where inelastic demand has kept sales high, the government will receive $9,000.

We can conclude that the lower the price elasticity of demand the greater the amount of tax revenues that will be collected.

THINK IT THROUGH: If demand is perfectly inelastic then it will be impossible for consumers to avoid the tax and tax revenues will be maximized. Thinking about the kinds of goods that might have an extremely inelastic demand, why do governments tend to shy away from this approach? Might many of those goods be necessities?

Employment Concerns: Frankly, politicians wish to remain in office and, to do so, their policies must appeal to voters. The imposition of a tax will raise the price of the taxed good, reduce the size of the market, and cause unemployment for workers in the industry. Politically, it is wise to tax foreign goods. If, however, we must tax a locally produced good, then what lessons does elasticity teach? Tax goods with an inelastic demand! In West Carolina, job loss will be small but East Carolina's job loss is likely to be quite severe.

Conclusion: Sales taxes can raise the greatest revenues and minimize job losses if levied on goods with a relatively inelastic demand. Politically, this is an attractive option. However, inelastic goods may be necessities for which there are few substitutes and taxes may therefore impose hardships. The policy maker would prefer to tax a good with an inelastic demand that is not a necessity. The ideal targets are inelastic goods that are addictive or detrimental in some way—"bads" such as cigarettes, alcohol, and gasoline. One argument for the legalization of marijuana is that the government would then be able to slap a tax on it!

Who Is Responsible for Gas Price Volatility?: Consumers habitually grumble about high gas prices, but also complain about the volatility of gas prices. Prices seem to fluctuate daily. Who is responsible for such volatile gas prices? The oil producers are among the "usual suspects" and, to be sure, oil supplies can be affected by political instability, and bad weather or other natural disasters. Oil companies, however, anticipate such occurrences and have inventories in hand to smooth out some of the fluctuations.

Assuming a given supply-side decrease, the reason for extreme movements in the market price must lie on the demand side of the market. In fact, the very inelasticity of demand is a prime reason for oil price elasticity. When we grumble about rapidly rising prices at the pumps, we should concede that the major culprit is the one whose hand is on the pump!

Review: In this chapter we have explored how economists quantify the relationship between price and quantity demanded, and what conclusions may be drawn from that information. In addition, other "elasticities" can be measured and these may be useful for managers seeking insight into future conditions in their own particular markets.

CHAPTER 5

Production, Costs, and Revenue

Perfect Competition in the Short Run

By the end of this chapter you will be able to:

1. Distinguish the short run from the long run.
2. Define marginal, total, and average product and explain the relationships between them.
3. State the law of diminishing marginal productivity and explain why it is a short-run law.
4. Explain how the specialization effect and congestion effect influence marginal productivity.
5. Define, distinguish, and explain the relationships among total cost, total fixed cost, and total variable cost; and among average total cost, average fixed cost, and average variable cost.
6. Define marginal cost and explain its behavior using your knowledge of marginal product.
7. Explain how the assumptions underlying the perfect competition model determine that the perfectly competitive firm will be a "price taker."
8. Define marginal revenue and explain why it is constant in perfect competition.
9. Define economic cost and economic profit and discuss the meaning of positive, zero, and negative economic profit.
10. State how firms determine the profit-maximizing level of output and explain why profit is maximized at that production level.

11. Explain what determines whether a firm should shut down or not shut down when short-run losses occur.

12. Explain why the marginal cost curve above the average variable cost curve is the firm's short-run supply curve.

Opening a company requires commitment, skill, and a product to sell. To make it survive and grow requires these same factors and also some luck. In April 2012, a new company, Balloonduck.com ("Twitter with questions"), opened up for business. As with any firm, Balloonduck's owners, two young entrepreneurs named Vivian Xue and Brandon Thornton, had already committed great energy, time, and expense into designing and financing their product. Will Balloonduck fly? Only time can tell but its owners have high hopes. Xue and Thornton will be faced with the same daily decisions and challenges as any other entrepreneur—Steve Jobs, Bill Gates, Sam Walton, Henry Ford—striving to make a profit. Decisions about hiring resources, resource mix, pricing, promotion, product development, and so on. Can economics offer insights?

Chapter Preview: This chapter moves from the decisions of utility-maximizing households to examine the behavior of profit-maximizing producers. In Chapter 4, while examining price elasticity of supply, we discovered that the ability of producers to respond to changes in prices is affected by the passage of time. We defined two conceptual time periods—the short run and the long run. In this chapter, we focus on production matters in the short-run time period. This chapter introduces many key economic topics—including productivity, costs, and economic profits—that will be reused in subsequent chapters.

Brain Teaser: Folk wisdom includes the sayings "there's no point crying over spilt milk," and "too many cooks spoil the broth." Both of these adages will be illustrated in this chapter. Spot them!

The Law of Diminishing Marginal Productivity: Production in the Short Run

Firms operate from day to day but also strategically. Although, as we saw in Chapter 4, these time periods are more conceptual than calendar in nature, the day-to-day functioning of a firm can be thought of as its "short run" operations whereas strategic planning is "long run."

In this initial section we introduce some new concepts and establish a basic law of production that governs the short-run behavior of any firm—large or small.

The Short Run and the Long Run—A Review

The **long run** is a period long enough for the firm to alter any and all of its factors of production—all resources are variable in the long run. In the short run at least one resource is not variable—at least one resource is fixed in quantity. In the **short run**, although resources can be used more or less intensively, the firm has a fixed scale of production. In the long run, new firms can enter or leave the market but, in the short run, they can't.

Learning Tip: The best way to distinguish between the short run and the long run is to understand the long run first. In the long run, the firm can adjust all of its resources. Put simply, the short run is anything less.

THINK IT THROUGH: As a student you resemble a firm. Your "product" is your grade (although educationalists would argue that it's your increased knowledge). With an exam approaching in one hour's time, how can you improve your grade? Most of your productive resources are fixed—the die is almost cast. With more time, more options open up—late night cramming, study groups, visits to your instructor during office hours. Unless your learning resources are completely unconstrained you are operating in the short run.

Production Concepts: A Family of Products

In our following discussion we examine the firm's output as it changes its usage of resources such as workers. It is assumed that each unit of labor (worker) is identical in quality. The same assumption is made for every class of resource—each unit of capital is identical in abilities. Is this true? Of course not, but removing this assumption would substantially complicate the analysis without significantly changing our conclusions.

First, consider a firm—Freda's Family Pies. Freda is operating in the short run—she has some variable resources (labor) and some fixed resources (her ovens and other capital stock, the premises she rents, and so on).

Total Product (TP) is the firm's total output. If we were to graph Freda's supply curve, then total product is identical to "quantity supplied" (q) on that diagram. The terms are interchangeable. Typically, we would expect total product to increase as more units of the variable resources are hired and combined with the fixed resources.

Consider Table 5-1, which shows how Freda's total product changes as additional workers are hired. With no workers, total product is zero— there is no one to operate the machines. This table is a production function.

Table 5-1. *Freda's Daily Production Function*

Number of Workers	Total Product
1	8
2	18
3	30
4	40
5	48
6	54
7	57
8	59
9	60
10	60

A **production function** shows the relationship between inputs and output. It can be represented as a table, a graph, or even as a mathematical equation, but, in essence, it simply shows total product at different levels of usage of the variable and fixed resources.

The production function can be shown graphically as in Figure 5-1. Total product (TP) is on the vertical axis and units of the variable resource, labor (L), are on the horizontal axis. The typical shape of a production is as shown—an elongated S-shape. The reason for this shape will be described below.

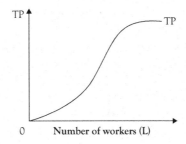

Figure 5-1. Freda's daily production function.

THINK IT THROUGH: The production function is drawn based on the assumption that only the number of workers changes. What would happen to the function if other production conditions change? For example, what would happen to the curve if labor productivity increased through a training program? The function must begin at the origin (no workers, no production). However, the function will become steeper as, at any other level of hiring, total product will be greater with more resources applied.

Average Product (AP) of a resource (labor, for example) is the total product divided by the number of units of that resource.

$$AP = TP/L = q/L$$

If Freda produces 40 pies and employs four workers, then the average product of labor is ten pies—each worker averages ten pies. We can calculate the average product for any resource; for example, if Freda has two ovens and produces 40 pies, then the average product of each oven is 20 pies.

Marginal Product (MP) of a resource (such as labor) is the change in total product divided by the change in the number of units of that resource.

$$MP = \Delta TP/\Delta L = \Delta q/\Delta L$$

We can see from Table 5-2 that, if Freda hires a fifth worker, total product increases by eight pies (from 40 to 48)—the marginal product of the

Table 5-2. The Relationship Between Total Product, Average Product, and Marginal Product

Number of Workers	Total Product	Average Product	Marginal Product
1	8	8.0	8
2	18	9.0	10
3	28	9.3	12
4	40	10.0	10
5	48	9.6	8
6	54	9.0	6
7	57	8.1	3
8	59	7.4	2
9	60	6.7	1
10	60	6.0	0

fifth worker is eight pies. The marginal product of the seventh worker is three pies—total product increases from 54 pies to 57 pies as the quantity of labor increases by one. The marginal product of the tenth worker is zero.

Comment: Mathematically, the relationship between marginal product and total product is exactly the same as the relationship we found between marginal utility and total utility. Marginal product is the derivative of the production function or, less technically, the slope of the production function.

Slope is "rise over run." In Figure 5-1, the "rise" is how much total product changed whereas the "run" is how much labor changes. With the tenth worker, when marginal product is zero, the change in total product, therefore, is zero.

The Behavior of Marginal Product: In our example, marginal product increases, peaks, decreases, and then becomes zero. This is the typical pattern of behavior for marginal product. Why? There are two conflicting effects occurring as additional workers are hired—the specialization effect and the congestion effect.

The Specialization Effect: In a very famous passage in *The Wealth of Nations*, Adam Smith described his visit to a factory making pins. The workers were practicing *division of labor*—each worker had an allotted specialized task and, Smith observed that, because of this, production levels were very high. He noted that, if each worker did all the tasks necessary to make a pin, moving from job to job, from location to location, and handling the variety of tools required, production would be low. Similarly, if two or more workers each followed the production of a pin through from start to finish, production would remain low. However, additional workers permit specialization and, in turn, specialization permits increased proficiency and decreased unproductive time between jobs.

The specialization effect occurs because, as extra workers are added, it becomes increasingly possible to split up tasks and to allocate and train workers to perform particular skills where their speed of operation can be increased and spoilage reduced. Through specialization, marginal productivity increases.

The Congestion Effect: Marginal productivity, however, can't increase indefinitely. In the short run, we have fixed constraints—a given number of machines or a given factory size, for instance. Eventually, with fewer machines or less workspace available for new workers, marginal productivity will decrease. In addition, worker concentration may decrease, discontent and low effort may increase, and repetitive motion injuries may become more prevalent. These elements are aspects of the **congestion effect**.

THINK IT THROUGH: Suppose we have a mechanic's garage with one inspection bay containing all the usual equipment. These are our fixed resources. If we hire one mechanic, he will be responsible for all the tasks. At any time, though, much of the equipment will be underutilized. A second mechanic permits specialization and teamwork—much more productive. A third mechanic may assist or relieve his co-workers and increase the number of work orders completed but, with only one bay and a limited number of tools, he may be underemployed as he waits for a necessary tool to become available. While a fourth worker still may contribute to getting jobs done a little faster, he could get in the way or start unproductive conversations. In fact, four workers milling around in a small space may not just be unproductive—it may be dangerous. The fifth worker is overkill: Too many cooks spoil the broth.

David Ricardo recognized this second, negative, effect of adding workers and coined the **Law of Diminishing Marginal Productivity**. This law states that, as equal units of a variable resource are added to a quantity of fixed resources, marginal productivity decreases after some point. The law applies only in the short run because, by definition, there are no fixed resources in the long run. If we see marginal productivity declining in the long run, then a different explanation will be required.

THINK IT THROUGH: After some point, marginal productivity decreases as more workers are hired. It is tempting, but incorrect, to assume that the productivity decline is because the new hires are somehow less talented than the first workers chosen. The law of diminishing marginal productivity specifies that the units are "equal" in ability and motivation. The productivity decline is due to the congestion effect, not because of a decline in the quality of the workers.

THINK IT THROUGH: "Speed dating," where singles assemble to meet each other for short periods, and possibly follow up afterwards, is related to the law of diminishing marginal productivity. After the initial few minutes of a traditional first date, time spent together yields sharply diminishing returns in terms of information gained with respect to whether an individual is worth following up whereas speed dating maximizes the exchange of important information in the minimum amount of time. "Speed networking" for business connections is a similar practice.

The reason that marginal product increases, reaches a maximum value, and then decreases is because of the interplay between the specialization effect and the congestion effect. Initially, with many unused fixed resources, the specialization effect dominates and marginal product increases, but, eventually, as workers jostle for fixed resources, the congestion effect wins the day and marginal product decreases. Marginal product could decrease to zero or, theoretically at least, become negative—hiring the additional worker would reduce total product!

The Shape of the Production Function: The interplay between the initially dominant specialization effect and the ultimately dominant congestion effect gives us the reason for the "elongated S" shape of the production function. Marginal product is the slope of the production function, so, as marginal product increases, the slope of the production function becomes steeper; as marginal product decreases, so the production function's slope becomes less steep until, when marginal

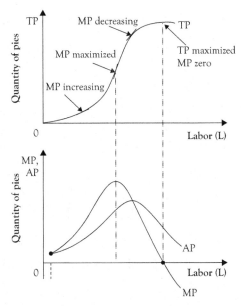

Figure 5-2. Relationships between total, average, and marginal product.

product is zero, total product is maximized. The relationship between marginal product and the slope of the production function is shown in Figure 5-2.

The relationship between marginal product and average product is governed by the **Average-Marginal Rule**, which pops up throughout your microeconomics course. If the marginal (extra) value exceeds the average, then the average will increase. For example, if your GPA is 3.0 and you earn an "A" in this course, then your average will rise. If the marginal value is less than the average, then the average will increase—a "D" in this course will make your average fall. If the marginal value equals the average, then the average will not change. Finally, for the first observation (the very first course you take in college), the marginal value and the average value must be equal.

In our example, the marginal product of Freda's first worker is eight pies—this must also be the first worker's average product. Because of the specialization effect, the second worker's marginal product exceeds that of the first, and this makes average product increase too. As marginal product declines, it drags down average product. The maximum value for average product must occur with the worker whose average product and marginal product are equal.

THINK IT THROUGH: If marginal product exceeds average product, then average product must be rising. If marginal product is less than average product, then average product must be falling. Average product, therefore, must neither be rising nor be falling—must be at its maximum—when marginal product is equal to it.

The Short-Run Cost Picture: Costs in the Short Run

Economic Cost: In economics, cost ultimately means opportunity cost—the value of the next most preferred alternative relinquished. For convenience, we will use dollars to measure cost throughout this chapter and the chapters that follow, but keep in mind that economic cost is a deeper concept. Recall, too, that, for an economist (but not for an accountant), costs include an adequate reward for the entrepreneur—a *normal profit* is included in economic cost.

THINK IT THROUGH: We examined this issue of a normal profit in Chapter 1, when we considered Juan, Carlos, and trading incentives. Revisit that example to review the link between normal profit and the entrepreneur's opportunity cost.

To see the distinction between accounting cost (which includes only the explicit payments made for the use of resources) and economic cost (which counts explicit costs *and* implicit costs), consider the following example. Asa, an accountant who earns $70,000 per year in salary and benefits, quits his job, and opens a firm selling environmentally friendly sandals. The sandals are a success! At the end of the year, after paying his workers, materials suppliers, and so on, Asa calculates his profit to be $25,000. His wife, Ella, who has an economics degree is not impressed and tells him that he has made an economic loss, the sandals firm is a failure, and that he should reapply for his old job. From Asa's viewpoint his income exceeded his outlays and, therefore, he made a profit. From Ella's viewpoint, Asa gave up $70,000 to make $25,000 and, therefore, he's $45,000 in the hole.

Total Variable Cost, Total Fixed Cost, and Total Cost

In the short run, a firm has some variable resources and at least one fixed resource. Accordingly, the firm also has variable costs and fixed costs. Labor is Freda's variable resource, which she hires at a wage rate of $30 per worker per day, and her ovens are her fixed resource—we assume that Freda is contractually obligated to rent the ovens at a charge of $25 per day per oven, for a period of time, whether or not she uses them.

Total Variable Cost (TVC) is the total cost of Freda's variable resources—in this example, her wage bill. When she hires no workers, Freda's wage bill is zero. With one worker, Freda will pay $30; with two, $60, and so on, as shown in Table 5-3. With nine workers, the total cost of Freda's variable resources will be $270.

Table 5-3. Freda's Total Costs and Marginal Cost

Number of Workers	Total Product	Marginal Product	Total Variable Cost	Total Fixed Cost	Total Cost	Marginal Cost
0	0	—	0	$50	$50	—
1	8	8	$30	$50	$80	30/8
2	18	10	$60	$50	$110	30/10
3	28	12	$90	$50	$140	30/12
4	40	10	$120	$50	$170	30/10
5	48	8	$150	$50	$200	30/8
6	54	6	$180	$50	$230	30/6
7	57	3	$210	$50	$260	30/3
8	59	2	$240	$50	$290	30/2
9	60	1	$270	$50	$320	30/1

We can graph total variable cost in Figure 5-3, with total variable costs on the vertical axis and total product (quantity) on the horizontal axis. When output is zero, Freda will reduce the amount of her variable resource to zero and her variable costs will be zero. After that, as output increases, total variable cost will increase as shown in Figure 5-3. As we shall see, the shape of the TVC curve is determined by the interplay of the specialization effect and the congestion effect.

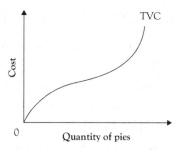

Figure 5-3. Total variable cost.

THINK IT THROUGH: How would the TVC function change if the wage increased to $40 per worker? At zero output (and zero workers), total variable cost would still be zero, but, as workers are hired, the wage bill would increase more rapidly than before—graphically, the TVC function would pivot upwards from the origin and become steeper. At 40 units of output and four workers, for instance, total variable cost would be $160 instead of $120.

Total Fixed Cost (TFC) is the total cost of Freda's fixed resources—in this example, her contractual payment for the ovens. Total fixed cost does not vary with output. If Freda produces no pies and the ovens are idle, she must still meet her obligation of $50 per day. If Freda produces 60 pies per day and the ovens are in continual use, her obligation remains at $50. Total Fixed Cost is constant as output changes as shown in Figure 5-4.

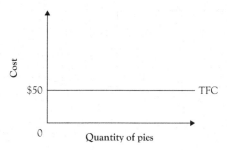

Figure 5-4. Total fixed cost.

Total Cost (TC) is the total cost of production—the sum of total variable cost and total fixed cost at each output level.

$$TC = TVC + TFC$$

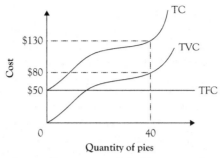

Figure 5-5. Total variable cost, total fixed cost, and total cost.

If Freda produces no pies, then her total cost will equal her total fixed cost. If she produces 40 pies, then total cost will be $170—$120 for the four workers and $50 for the ovens. Freda's Total Cost curve is shown in Figure 5-5.

Comment: Note that the slope of the TC function and that of the TVC function are identical. Because total fixed cost doesn't change as output level changes, only total variable cost affects the behavior of total cost as output changes. In addition, at each output level, the vertical distance between the TC function and the TVC function is constant—it's the unchanging value of total fixed cost.

Marginal Cost (MC) is the change in total cost caused by the production of one additional unit of output. More generally,

$$MC = \Delta TC/\Delta TP = \Delta TC/\Delta q$$

If Freda's fourth worker increases total cost by $30 and increases output by 10 units, then the marginal cost of each of those units is $3.00. In Table 5-4, the marginal cost values are presented conventionally but, in Table 5-3, the marginal cost values are presented as fractions. By inspection, we see that marginal cost decreases as output level initially increases but then starts to increase—a U-shaped curve, as shown in Figure 5-6. Why does marginal cost have a U-shaped curve? Consider the fractional values. The numerator is constant ($30) and is equal to the change in total variable cost, so any variation must derive from the denominator. Note that the values in the denominator are the values for marginal product. Marginal cost can be expressed as

$$MC = \Delta TVC/ MP$$

Table 5-4. *Freda's Average Costs and Marginal Cost*

Number of Workers	Total Product	Marginal Product	Marginal Cost	Average Variable Cost	Average Fixed Cost	Average Total Cost
0	0	—	—	—	—	—
1	8	8	$3.75	$3.75	$6.25	$10.00
2	18	10	$3.00	$3.33	$2.78	$6.11
3	30	12	$2.50	$3.00	$1.67	$5.00
4	40	10	$3.00	$3.00	$1.25	$4.25
5	48	8	$3.75	$3.13	$1.04	$4.17
6	54	6	$5.00	$3.33	$0.93	$4.26
7	57	3	$10.00	$3.68	$0.88	$4.56
8	59	2	$15.00	$4.07	$0.85	$4.92
9	60	1	$30.00	$4.50	$0.83	$5.33

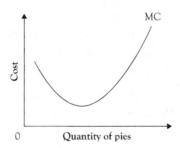

Figure 5-6. *Marginal cost.*

Marginal cost decreases as marginal product increases and increases as marginal product decreases. When marginal product is maximized, with the third worker, marginal cost is minimized. Ultimately, the behavior of marginal cost is due to the struggle between the specialization effect and the congestion effect. Initially, with the specialization effect dominant, marginal cost decreases, but, eventually, with the congestion effect dominant, marginal cost increases.

Average Variable Cost, Average Fixed Cost, and Average Total Cost

Average Variable Cost (AVC) is total variable cost divided by quantity (or total product). When 40 pies are produced, total variable cost is $120 and average variable cost is $3.00. See Table 5-04 for the other values.

$$AVC = TVC/q$$

Average variable cost graphs as a U-shaped curve. This shape follows from the average-marginal rule that we saw earlier in this chapter. Note that, for the first batch of pies produced, average variable cost equals marginal cost at $3.75 per pie. This is no accident. The rule states that, for the first observation, the marginal value and the average value must be equal— both marginal cost and average variable cost are associated with total variable cost. See Figure 5-7. After the first observation, marginal cost decreases, which pulls down the associated average variable cost. Eventually, marginal cost increases, becoming greater than average variable cost, therefore making average variable cost increase. When marginal cost and average variable cost are equal, average variable cost is minimized. As with marginal cost, average variable cost's shape is due to the interaction of the specialization and congestion effects.

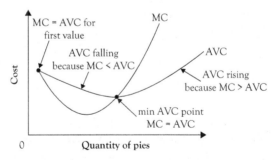

Figure 5-7. The relationship between marginal cost and average variable cost.

Average Fixed Cost (AFC) is total fixed cost divided by quantity (or total product). When 40 pies are produced, total fixed cost is $50 and average fixed cost is $1.25. As output increases, overhead costs are spread over greater numbers of units, and average fixed cost decreases. See Table 5-4 for the other values.

$$AFC = TFC/q$$

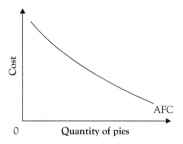

Figure 5-8. Average fixed cost.

Average fixed cost graphs as a continually downward sloping curve—a rectangular hyperbola—as shown in Figure 5-8. (A rectangular hyperbola has the same area under the curve at all points.) The AFC curve cannot become zero, because, if it did, this would imply that total fixed costs also were zero.

Average Total Cost (ATC) is total cost divided by quantity (or total product). When 40 pies are produced, total cost is $170 and average total cost is $4.25. See Table 5-04 for the other values.

$$ATC = TC/q = TVC/q + TFC/q$$

or

$$ATC = AVC + AFC$$

Average total cost (the sum of average variable cost and average fixed cost) graphs as a U-shaped curve. As output expands, both AVC and AFC decrease—ATC must decrease. Eventually, though, AVC starts to increase and, despite AFC's continuing decline, this causes ATC to increase. The intersection of the AVC function and the AFC function determines the output level where average total cost is minimized. See Figure 5-9.

We can explain ATC's U-shaped appearance differently. Marginal cost is the addition to total cost caused by an extra unit of production. We can see that, initially, marginal cost is less than average total cost—we are reminded by the average-marginal rule that average total cost must decrease. Eventually, however, marginal cost increases, becoming greater

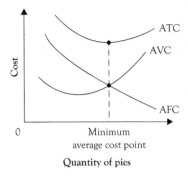

Figure 5-9. Relationships between average variable cost, average fixed cost, and average total cost.

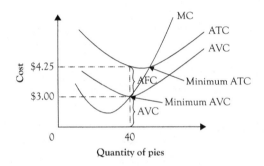

Figure 5-10. Relationships between marginal cost, average variable cost, and average total cost.

than average total cost and making average total cost increase. When marginal cost and average total cost are equal, average total cost is minimized.

Comment: As we saw with average variable cost, average total cost's behavior is due to marginal cost and, therefore, the interplay of the specialization and congestion effects. Figure 5-10 illustrates the relationships between average variable cost, average total cost, and marginal cost.

Note that average fixed cost is represented in the diagram. The vertical "gap" between ATC and AVC at a given output level is AFC—when 40 pies are produced, ATC is $4.25, AVC is $3.00, and AFC is $1.25. This gap decreases as output level increases because average fixed cost decreases as output expands.

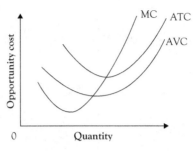

Figure 5-11. The firm's short-run cost picture.

Short-run Cost Picture: We may call Figure 5-11 the firm's "short-run cost picture" and it is an important diagram to understand fully. The relationships represented—a union of economics and mathematics—are true for any firm in the short run, whether large or small, competitive or monopolistic. When we refer to cost in economics, in the end analysis we mean opportunity cost, so, to remind ourselves of this point, the vertical axis is labeled "opportunity cost." In the final analysis, this diagram looks the way it does because of the interaction of the specialization and congestion effects.

THINK IT THROUGH: As output expands, the ATC curve and the AVC curve seem to converge. Can they ever touch (or intersect)? The ATC curve and the AVC curve cannot touch or intersect. The difference between ATC and AVC is average fixed cost and, although it diminishes as output increases, AFC can never be zero. If you are unsure on this point, please review the "Costs" section.

Comment: We have spent considerable time building up the "short-run cost picture" because it is so important to our understanding of what follows. You should review all of the previous definitions and diagrams—and see how they interact—before continuing.

It is crucial that you can interpret and draw this diagram correctly. It's not merely a collection of randomly positioned curves. The marginal cost curve must intersect the AVC curve and ATC curve at their minimum value. The easiest way to draw the diagram correctly is to draw the MC curve first, then the ATC curve, making sure that the ATC curve bottoms out when it meets the MC curve. Finally, add the AVC curve—it also bottoms out when it reaches the MC curve. The AVC curve approaches the

ATC curve as output increases because average fixed cost (the difference between ATC and AVC, that is, AFC) decreases.

The "Revenue" Picture for a Perfectly Competitive Firm

Just as we can derive the firm's "short-run cost picture," we can derive its "revenue picture." However, the firm's revenue picture depends on the sort of industry within which it operates. "Perfect competition," a theoretical ideal rather than a form of industry to be found in the real world, is the workhorse of microeconomics and the standard against which the performance of other forms of industrial organization are measured.

Characteristics of a Perfectly Competitive Industry

A perfectly competitive industry contains many small firms, each producing a homogeneous (standardized) product with free entry into, and exit from, the market in the long run. Further, it is assumed that buyers have complete knowledge about the quality of the product and the market price. A seller can't deceive a buyer into paying a higher than market price by claiming that his product is superior to that of his rivals—the buyer knows that claim isn't true. No individual firm has any control over the price it receives for its product—each firm is a price taker. These assumptions lead to an important implication. Each firm faces a perfectly elastic (horizontal) demand curve.

It is difficult to find examples of such an industry in today's world although agricultural products may come close. Farms produce two billion bushels of wheat annually, with each farm dependent on the market price. In perfectly competitive markets, the individual firm has nothing to advertise—no lower price, no "new improved" quality, or better service, but we might expect marketing boards (eggs, wheat, potatoes) and industry-funded advertising intended to stimulate demand for the product, such as the California Raisins or "Beef—it's what's for dinner!". Such industries may get close to perfect competition.

The Firm's Revenue Picture

Average Revenue and Marginal Revenue: Let us suppose that Phoebe's Fine Fruit-Filled Pies (a rival of Freda's Fruit Pies) operates in a perfectly competitive market and that the market price of a fruit pie, determined by market demand and market supply, is $5.00, as shown in the left-hand panel of Figure 5-12. At that price, the quantity demanded for Phoebe's pies is as great or as small as Phoebe wishes it to be. In the right-hand panel, Phoebe's demand curve is shown as horizontal; she faces a perfectly elastic demand for her product.

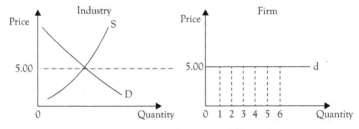

Figure 5-12. The demand curve faced by a perfectly competitive firm.

In Chapter 4, we saw that **Total Revenue** (TR) is total spending by consumers or, from the seller's viewpoint, total income received—either way, price × quantity. See Table 5-5.

Table 5-5. Phoebe's Average Revenue and Marginal Revenue

Price	Quantity Demanded	Total Revenue	Average Revenue	Marginal Revenue
$10.00	0	0	–	–
$10.00	1	$10.00	$10.00	$10.00
$10.00	2	$20.00	$10.00	$10.00
$10.00	3	$30.00	$10.00	$10.00
$10.00	4	$40.00	$10.00	$10.00
$10.00	5	$50.00	$10.00	$10.00
$10.00	6	$60.00	$10.00	$10.00
$10.00	7	$70.00	$10.00	$10.00
$10.00	8	$80.00	$10.00	$10.00

Average Revenue (AR) is total revenue per unit or, simply, price. The terms "price" and "average revenue" can be used interchangeably—this is *always* true.

$$AR = TR/q = (P \times q)/q = P$$

If Phoebe sells four pies at $10 each, her total revenue is $40 and her average revenue is $10 ($40/4).

Marginal Revenue (MR) is defined as by how much total revenue changes when an extra unit is sold.

$$MR = \Delta TR/\Delta q$$

In perfect competition, marginal revenue equals price or average revenue—each extra unit sold increases total revenue by the amount of the price. Phoebe's demand curve is also her marginal revenue curve.

THINK IT THROUGH: In perfect competition, average revenue must equal marginal revenue. Marginal revenue is change in total revenue divided by change in quantity. Any change in total revenue must be caused either by a "change in price" or by a "change in quantity." However, because the firm is a price taker, price does *not* change as the firm's output level changes. Therefore, the only way that total revenue can change is through a change in quantity. The marginal revenue formula becomes

$$MR = (P \times \Delta q)/\Delta q = P$$

THINK IT THROUGH: Another way to think about the relationship between average revenue and marginal revenue is through the average-marginal rule. We know that average revenue is constant—it's a horizontal line. If marginal revenue were greater than average revenue, then average revenue would increase and, if marginal revenue were less than average revenue then average revenue would decrease. Since average revenue neither increases nor decreases as output increases, marginal revenue *must* equal average revenue.

If Phoebe sells a fifth pie, her total revenue increases to $50, a change in total revenue of $10 for a change in quantity of one unit.

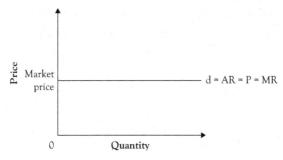

Figure 5-13. The firm's revenue picture.

The firm's horizontal demand curve is also average revenue (price) and marginal revenue, as shown in Figure 5-13. This single line is the "revenue picture" for a perfectly competitive firm.

Comment: The perfectly competitive firm's "revenue picture" may look deceptively simple, but it contains several key ideas, most particularly that of marginal revenue. In the next section we combine the firm's "short-run cost picture" and its "revenue picture" to analyze how the firm responds in the light of changing prices.

Profit Maximization: Four Short-Run Cases

We assume that the firm is in business to maximize profit. Can we devise rules to guide the firm's behavior? Our conclusion will be that, with one exception, the profit-maximizing firm should produce at the output level at which marginal revenue equals marginal cost. The profit-maximizing condition, then, is MR = MC.

Economic Profit

Total economic profit, the difference between total revenue and total cost, is positive when total revenue exceeds total cost and is negative when total revenue is less than total cost. When total revenue equals total cost, then the firm is breaking even.

Total Economic Profit = Total Revenue − Total Cost

The firm's goal is to maximize total economic profit. Because its price is determined by market forces, the only choice variable for the perfectly competitive firm is output level. Consider Figure 5-14, which shows marginal revenue and marginal cost for Phoebe's Fine Fruit-Filled Pies, a perfectly competitive firm.

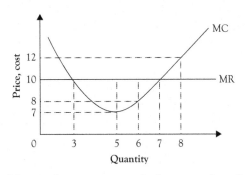

Figure 5-14. Marginal revenue, marginal cost, and profit maximization.

The Profit-Maximizing Rule

Phoebe's price is $10 per pie as set by the market. Her marginal revenue, therefore, is also $10 per pie. Figure 5-14 includes a U-shaped marginal cost curve. Phoebe will maximize her profit by producing seven pies, where marginal revenue equals marginal cost (MR = MC). Should Phoebe produce the fifth pie? Yes, because if she does, then the fifth pie will bring in $3.00 in extra profits. For the same reason, she should also produce the sixth pie, which increases profits by $2.00 (the difference between marginal revenue and marginal cost is +$2.00). She should *not* produce the eighth pie, which reduces profits by $2.00 (the difference between marginal revenue and marginal cost is −$2.00).

We can conclude that, when marginal revenue exceeds marginal cost, output should be increased—the marginal unit brings in more revenue than it costs. When marginal revenue is less than marginal cost, output should be decreased—the marginal unit costs more than it earns in revenue. Production level, then, will adjust until marginal revenue and marginal cost are equal. The rule for profit maximization is to produce up to the point where

MR = MC

This conclusion—that the profit-maximizing output level occurs when MR = MC—is an important one and holds for any firm in any kind of industry, not just for perfect competitive firms. There are, however, two exceptions, one of which (the "shutdown" case) we address later in this chapter and the other we address now.

Recall that the MC curve is U-shaped. Because of this, marginal revenue and marginal cost are equal at two output levels—three pies and seven pies in Figure 5-14. There is, however, one unique profit-maximizing output level—seven pies. Producing only three pies will not maximize profit; in fact, it will maximize losses! We can make our profit-maximization rule unambiguous by stating that we should produce up to the point where

MR = MC (and MC is increasing)

THINK IT THROUGH: Consider the relationship between marginal revenue and marginal cost. For each unit produced until the third pie, the extra cost incurred exceeds the extra revenue earned—each of these pies is losing money for the firm. If Phoebe sets production at three pies, she will have nothing but losses. By expanding production to units where marginal revenue exceeds marginal cost, her profitability is improved—and maximized with the seventh pie.

Four Short-Run Cases

Overview: In the short run, the manager of a profit-maximizing firm may encounter four situations—economic profit may be positive, zero, or negative. (This may seem like three situations but, as we shall see, it is four!)

Referring to our formula for total economic profit

$$\text{Total Economic Profit} = \text{Total Revenue} - \text{Total Cost}$$
$$= (P \times q) - (ATC \times q)$$
$$= (P - ATC)q$$

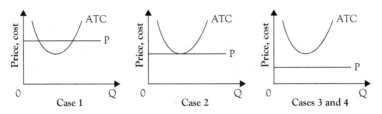

Figure 5-15. Relationships between price and average total cost.

Total economic profit is determined by the relationship between price and average total cost—price can exceed, equal, or be less than average total cost, as shown in Figure 5-15. Graphically, if the horizontal price line cuts through the ATC curve, then the firm can earn an economic profit. If the price line touches the ATC curve at that curve's minimum point, then the firm can earn break even and earn zero economic profit. If the price line entirely misses the ATC curve, then the firm must earn a negative economic profit (in other words, an economic loss).

Case 1: Positive Economic Profit

When the product's price exceeds average total cost, then the firm can earn an economic profit. Following our profit-maximizing rule, the firm should produce at q* (where MR = MC). At this output level, the difference between price and average total cost (P − ATC) represents the economic profit per unit. Multiplying by the number of units gives us the total economic profit.

Table 5-6 and Figure 5-16 provide information for Fenella's Famous Fruit Pies. For simplicity, we assume that Fenella must hire each worker for the entire day. At a price of $6.00 per pie, marginal revenue equals marginal cost when 68 pies are produced.

Total economic profit = (P − ATC)q*
                     = ($6.00 − $3.26) 68
                     = $186.32 ($186.00 when corrected for
                       rounding error)

Total economic profit is calculated in Table 5-6 and is represented by the shaded area in Figure 5-16.

Table 5-6. Profit Maximization when Price is $6.00 per Pie

Total Product	Marginal Cost	Average Total Cost	Total Cost	Marginal Revenue (Price)	Total Revenue	Total Economic Profit
0	–	–	$30	$6.00	0	–$30
6	$4.00	$9.00	$54	$6.00	$36	–$18
14	$3.00	$5.57	$78	$6.00	$84	$6
24	$2.40	$4.25	$102	$6.00	$144	$42
40	$1.50	$3.15	$126	$6.00	$240	$114
50	$2.40	$3.00	$150	$6.00	$300	$150
58	$3.00	$3.00	$174	$6.00	$348	$174
64	$4.00	$3.09	$198	$6.00	$384	$186
68	$6.00	$3.26	$222	$6.00	$408	$186
71	$8.00	$3.46	$246	$6.00	$426	$180

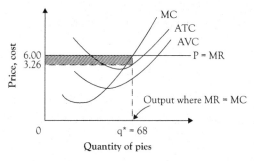

Figure 5-16. Case 1: positive economic profit.

THINK IT THROUGH: Total economic profit = $(P - ATC)q^*$. Alternatively, it is the difference between total revenue and total cost. Verify that the difference between total revenue and total cost is $186. You can use this alternative method for the following cases too.

THINK IT THROUGH: In the final column of the table, profit is maximized at *two* output levels, 64 pies and 68 pies. Why does this happen and which output level should we choose? We should choose the output level at which marginal revenue and marginal cost are equal. When marginal revenue and marginal cost are equal, it is inevitable that two output levels will render the same amount of profit because marginal revenue indicates how much total revenue has changed whereas marginal cost indicates how much total cost has changed. When marginal revenue and marginal cost are equal, the change in total revenue and total cost must be equal, meaning that the difference between them (total economic profit) is not changed as output level moves, in this case, from 64 pies to 68 pies.

Case 2: Zero Economic Profit—The Break-Even Case

When the product's price equals average total cost, then the firm breaks even and earns zero economic profit. The firm should still follow the profit-maximizing rule and produce at where MR = MC. At this output level, the difference between price and average total cost (P − ATC) is zero. Choosing any other output level, an economic loss will be suffered because price lies below average total cost.

Table 5-7 and Figure 5-17 consider Fenella's Famous Fruit Pies when the market price is $3.00 per pie. Marginal revenue equals marginal cost when 58 pies are produced.

$$\text{Total economic profit} = (P - ATC)q^*$$
$$= (\$3.00 - \$3.00)\,58$$
$$= \$0.00$$

Total economic profit is calculated in Table 5-7.

Table 5-7. Profit Maximization when Price is $3.00 per Pie

Total Product	Marginal Cost	Average Total Cost	Total Cost	Marginal Revenue (Price)	Total Revenue	Total Economic Profit
0	–	–	$30	$3.00	0	−$30
6	$4.00	$9.00	$54	$3.00	$18	−$36
14	$3.00	$5.57	$78	$3.00	$42	−$36
24	$2.40	$4.25	$102	$3.00	$72	−$30
40	$1.50	$3.15	$126	$3.00	$120	−$6
50	$2.40	$3.00	$150	$3.00	$150	$0
58	$3.00	$3.00	$174	$3.00	$174	$0
64	$4.00	$3.09	$198	$3.00	$192	−$6
68	$6.00	$3.26	$222	$3.00	$204	−$18
71	$8.00	$3.46	$246	$3.00	$213	−$23

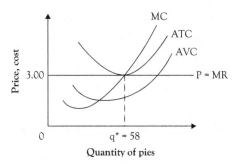

Figure 5-17. Case 2: zero economic profit.

Comment: In this situation it is tempting, but incorrect, to conclude that the entrepreneur should close down because "she is not making a profit." But she *is* making a profit! Recall that economic cost incorporates payments to *all* resources, including an adequate rate of return—a normal profit—for the entrepreneur. In this situation the entrepreneur certainly is not earning any extra profit, but she is earning enough profit to wish to stay in business.

Case 3: Negative Economic Profit but Continuing to Produce

When the product's price is less than average total cost, then the firm must suffer an economic loss. Why doesn't the firm raise its price? It can't—it's a "price taker." The firm must decide whether or not to continue production in the short run. The best option depends on whether the firm minimizes its losses by producing or by not producing. The latter option is known as the "shutdown" case. In the short run, the firm has both fixed and variable resources and, therefore, fixed and variable costs. If its price is high enough to cover its operating expenses (its variable costs) then it should continue to produce but, if its price is so low that variable resources can't pay for their keep, then the firm should close its doors. The distinction between the two cases is the relationship between price and average variable cost.

If, at the output level where marginal revenue equals marginal cost, price equals or exceeds average variable cost, then production should occur.

Table 5-8. Profit Maximization when Price is $2.40 per Pie

Total Product	Marginal Cost	Average Total Cost	Average Variable Cost	Total Cost	Marginal Revenue (Price)	Total Revenue	Total Economic Profit
0	—	—	—	$30	$2.40	0	−$30.00
6	$4.00	$9.00	$4.00	$54	$2.40	$14.40	−$39.60
14	$3.00	$5.57	$3.43	$78	$2.40	$33.60	−$44.40
24	$2.40	$4.25	$3.00	$102	$2.40	$57.60	−$44.40
40	$1.50	$3.15	$2.40	$126	$2.40	$96.00	−$30.00
50	$2.40	$3.00	$2.40	$150	$2.40	$120.00	−$30.00
58	$3.00	$3.00	$2.48	$174	$2.40	$139.20	−$34.80
64	$4.00	$3.09	$2.62	$198	$2.40	$153.60	−$44.40
68	$6.00	$3.26	$2.82	$222	$2.40	$163.20	−$58.80
71	$8.00	$3.46	$3.04	$246	$2.40	$170.40	−$75.60

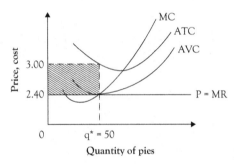

Figure 5-18. Case 3: negative economic profit but continuing to produce.

Table 5-8 and Figure 5-18 provide information for Fenella's Famous Fruit Pies when the price of a pie is $2.40. At a price of $2.40 per pie, marginal revenue equals marginal cost when 50 pies are produced.

$$\text{Total economic profit} = (P - ATC)q^*$$
$$= (\$2.40 - \$3.00)\,50$$
$$= -\$30.00$$

Total economic profit (a loss in this case) is calculated in Table 5-8 and is represented by the shaded area in Figure 5-18. Fennella's total fixed cost is $30 so, if she chooses to close down, her total economic loss would still be $30 as she would not be bringing in any revenue but would still be responsible for paying for her fixed resources. At any price equal to or above the minimum value for average variable cost, production should proceed because the producer can fully pay the variable resources and may have additional revenues that can defray some of the fixed expenses.

Case 4: Negative Economic Profit—The Shutdown Case

When the product's price is less than average variable cost, the firm should cease operations. There is no point hiring resources that can't pay their way. Because the firm's total revenues are zero and its total costs are only its total fixed cost, then its total economic loss will equal its total fixed cost.

If, at the output level where marginal revenue equals marginal cost, price equals or exceeds average variable cost, then production should occur.

General Procedure for Short-Run Profit Maximization

Overview: We are now in a position to develop a step-by-step procedure to maximize short-run profits or to minimize short-run losses for any firm, whether perfectly competitive or not.

Step 1: Find the output level (q*) at which marginal revenue equals marginal cost (and marginal cost is rising).

Step 2: At this output level, determine the difference between price (P) and average total cost (ATC). (P − ATC) is the per unit economic profit (or economic loss if ATC is the larger).

Step 3: Multiply (P − ATC) by q* to calculate the total economic profit (or loss).

However, when the firm is suffering a loss, we must consider the shutdown case.

Step 4: When a loss is being made, if the price is less than the average variable cost (P < AVC) then the firm should shut down. Its total economic loss will equal its total fixed cost.

The Perfectly Competitive Firm's Short-Run Supply Curve

We are now able to derive the firm's short-run supply curve. First, consider the firm's short-run cost picture as shown in Figure 5-19. We now

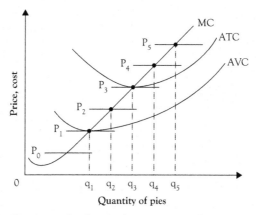

Figure 5-19. Deriving the firm's short-run supply curve.

superimpose the firm's revenue picture. (For visual effect, the horizontal price (marginal revenue) curves are shortened.)

At a price of P_0, no output will be produced, because this is the shutdown case—price is less than average variable cost. When the price rises to price of P_1, we are in a loss-minimizing "Case 3" situation and the firm will produce price of q_1 units of output. At P_2, we are still in a loss-minimizing situation and the firm will produce price of q_2 units of output in order to minimize losses. If the price is P_3, the firm is break-ing even ("Case 2") and will produce price of q_3 units of output. The firm will be able to earn economic profits at any price higher than P_3. At P_4, for instance, output will be q_4, while it will rise to q_5 if the price rises to P_5.

A firm's supply curve depicts how quantity supplied changes as price changes, and this is exactly what is shown here for any price equal to or greater than P_1. As we see in Figure 5-20, the firm's short-run supply curve *is* its marginal cost curve at and above the minimum point on the average variable cost curve and the market supply curve is the sum of the marginal cost curves for the firms in the industry.

THINK IT THROUGH: We reached this same conclusion about the relation-ship between supply and marginal cost, albeit by a different route, in Chapter 3 when examining Eve's supply of apples.

THINK IT THROUGH: What would happen to the position of the marginal cost curve (and, therefore, to the supply curve) if the firm was required to

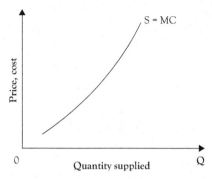

Figure 5-20. The firm's short-run supply curve.

pay its variable resource, workers, a higher wage? We know that marginal cost is affected by the change in total variable cost and that total variable cost will increase more rapidly if the wage increases. A higher wage will make the MC curve shift upwards. This translates into a decrease in supply (a leftward shift of the supply curve).

THINK IT THROUGH MORE: What would happen to the position of the marginal cost curve (and, therefore, to the supply curve) if the firm were required to pay more for a fixed resource? Nothing! First, fixed cost *can* change—it's the resource that is fixed, not the cost of using it. However, a change in fixed cost does not affect the rate of change in total cost—which is marginal cost. If you're unsure about this result, revisit Figure 5-05 and see what happens to the slope of the TC curve when the TFC curve shifts upwards.

Comment: Variable costs, not fixed costs, determine how a firm will respond to the market price. Fixed costs are "spilt milk."

THINK IT THROUGH (EVEN MORE): In Chapter 2, we listed the factors that can shift the position of the supply curve. Now we know that the supply curve is the marginal cost curve. Revisit the list and see if you can interpret how changes in those factors affect marginal cost. Hint: Keep in mind that marginal cost is, at heart, opportunity cost.

Unfinished business from Chapter 3: When we considered Eve's supply of apples, we noted that the marginal cost curve determined the lowest price Eve would accept for each apple. While this remains generally true, the shutdown case requires us to remark that, if price falls too low (i.e., below average variable cost) then Eve will produce no apples.

Also note that, although producer surplus is very similar to short-run total economic profit, they are not identical, because producer surplus fails to take account of fixed costs.

Review: This has been a long and complex chapter, containing many new and important concepts that will continue to be used in future chapters. Chief among these is the very concept of perfect competition—this theoretical ideal will be used in Chapter 6 to derive a yardstick against which to assess other forms of market organization.

CHAPTER 6

Perfect Competition in the Long Run

By the end of this chapter you will be able to:

1. Explain why the long-run average cost curve is U-shaped and give examples of factors that would cause economies or diseconomies of scale.
2. Outline the process by which long-run competitive equilibrium is achieved.
3. Indicate the long-run equilibrium profit-maximizing level of production.
4. List the performance criteria that hold in the perfectly competitive long-run equilibrium model and indicate how perfect competition results in efficient production.
5. Define allocative (Pareto) efficiency and explain why a perfectly competitive economy allocates resources efficiently, distributes outputs efficiently, and achieves the optimal output mix.
6. Identify two major causes of market failure and their consequences.

There is an old joke about an Economics professor (Ed) and a Business professor (Bob) who are walking along, with Ed a few steps ahead of his colleague. Each sees a $20 bill lying on the sidewalk. Ed walks past the bill but Bob swoops down and claims it. "Why didn't you grab the Jackson?" he asks. "Because, logically, it shouldn't be there!" replies Ed.

Used to thinking about the long run, the economist realizes that, in the long run, the bill will be picked up. His colleague recognizes a short-run profit opportunity when he sees it! Note, though, that after Bob acts, the profit opportunity disappears and the validity of Ed's assumption is restored.

Chapter Preview: In Chapter 5 we examined short-run production conditions and then turned our attention to the decisions faced by a perfectly competitive entrepreneur operating in the short run. We adopt the same approach in this chapter, but for the long run. Also, we establish "performance criteria" for an industry in long-run equilibrium and revisit the concept of efficiency that we first met in Chapter 1 but explored more comprehensively in Chapter 3.

Brain Teaser: It has been reported recently that emus have been roaming wild in Texas, set free by disillusioned farmers. Emus, of course, are not native to North America. Where have they come from, and why have they been liberated? The answers to these questions are provided in this chapter.

Economies and Diseconomies of Scale

As we saw in Chapter 5, in the short run the firm must deal with the production constraints caused by fixed resources. In the long run, however, there are no fixed resources—all resources are variable. The short-run distinction between average total cost and average variable cost vanishes in the long-run context. In the short run, because of the interplay between the specialization effect and the congestion effect, the firm experiences a U-shaped average total cost (ATC) curve. But what happens to costs when those fixed constraints are no longer present? In this section we'll find out.

Long-Run Costs

What does the firm's long-run average cost (LRAC) curve look like? To get an understanding of the long run we must, paradoxically, begin with the short run. From Chapter 5, we know that the firm's short-run average total cost (ATC) curve is U-shaped—because it is constrained by its fixed resources.

Suppose that the firm is a textile mill and the number of looms is its fixed resource. With 10 looms, its short-run ATC curve (ATC_{10}) might appear as shown in Figure 6-1.

However, if the firm has 20 looms, what can we say about the position of its short-run ATC curve? (You may object that the firm can't adjust the quantity of its fixed resource. This is true, of course, in the short run, but

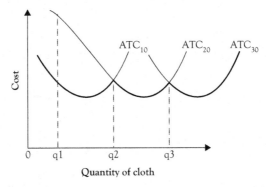

Figure 6-1. Deriving the firm's long-run average cost (LRAC) curve.

not in the long run. If it is valid to consider the firm's ATC curve with ten looms, then it is equally valid to consider its ATC curve with 20 looms.) The ATC curve will still be U-shaped, but the output level at which average total cost is minimized will be greater—visually, ATC_{20} will be farther to the right than ATC_{10}.

THINK IT THROUGH: Why will ATC_{20} be farther to the right than ATC_{10}? The output level at which the short-run average total cost is minimized is determined by the relative strengths of the specialization effect and the congestion effect. When the quantity of fixed resources is comparatively small, the congestion effect becomes dominant quite quickly but, with a greater amount of fixed resources, the specialization effect can dominate for a larger range of output levels before being overwhelmed by the congestion effect.

THINK IT THROUGH MORE: An alternative way to grasp why the minimum point for ATC_{20} must lie to the right of that for ATC_{10} is to consider average total cost when output level is very low. In such a situation, fixed costs are comparatively low if the firm has ten looms, but, if it has 20 looms, those overhead costs will be higher. The ATC_{20} curve starts at a level of fixed cost because so many of its fixed resources are being underused.

Figure 6-1 also shows the average total cost curve (ATC_{30}) if the firm has 30 looms. Again, the curve should be farther to the right because, with additional fixed resources, the deleterious consequences of the congestion effect can be staved off until greater levels of output.

The ATC curves are all drawn with the minimum costs at the same level bit. Is this likely? We'll address this issue when we look at economies and diseconomies of scale.

If the entrepreneur expects to produce only small amounts of cloth (for example, q_1 on the diagram), then, to reduce costs, he should buy only ten looms. For example, at q_1 units of output, short-run ATC is less with ten looms than with twenty or thirty looms. As output increases from q_1, the firm will move along ATC_{10}. After q_2 units of output the low-cost option is to increase the number of looms to 20. In the short run, this change is not possible but, in the long run, it is. Similarly, as output continues to expand, the firm's costs will move along ATC_{20} until q_3 is reached. After q_3, the firm should switch to having 30 looms. Again, in the short run it can't but, in the long run, it can.

The firm is not restricted to 10, 20, or 30 looms—it could have 15 looms or 25 looms, for instance—and each choice would have its own short-run ATC curve.

Given the long-run freedom to change the number of looms and all other resources, the firm's average cost curve in the long run is composed of the lowest portions of the family of all short-run ATC curves. At the limit, the LRAC curve is as shown in Figure 6-2—a horizontal line.

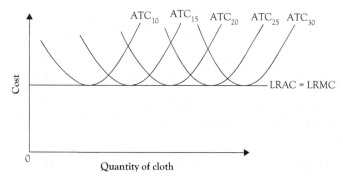

Figure 6-2. The firm's LRAC curve without economies and diseconomies of scale.

THINK IT THROUGH: The firm faces fewer constraints in the long run than in the short run; therefore, it makes sense that its long-run costs will be no higher than its short-run costs.

THINK IT THROUGH MORE: In Figure 6-2, the LRAC curve is a horizontal line. We know, therefore, that the long-run marginal cost (LRMC) curve must be that same horizontal line. Why? Recall the average-marginal rule from Chapter 5, which stated that, "if the marginal value exceeds the average, then the average will rise..." and so on. (Review this now if you don't remember.) In this case, the average value (LRAC) is neither increasing nor decreasing, which must mean that the marginal value is equal to it, in exactly the same way that average revenue and marginal revenue are equal for the perfectly competitive firm.

Economies of Scale and Diseconomies of Scale

As shown in Figure 6-2, the LRAC curve is horizontal, but is it probable, as the firm expands its scale of operations, that its average costs remain unchanged? Economists are divided on this point, but the prevailing view is that the LRAC curve is U-shaped, with long-run average costs decreasing as output level increases and then, after some point, increasing, as shown in Figure 6-3.

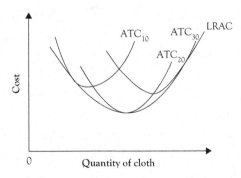

Figure 6-3. The U-shaped "envelope" curve.

We can see why the LRAC curve is sometimes called the "envelope curve," as it envelops all of the short-run average total cost curves. In fact, because its U-shape makes it look like a short-run average total cost curve, it is inviting to think that its behavior is shaped by the same forces—the specialization effect and the congestion effect—but this is not the case because these are short-run effects resulting from the presence of fixed resources.

The LRAC curve is downward sloping because of the dominant presence of economies of scale. **Economies of scale** (or increasing returns to scale) occur when an increase in the firm's scale of production causes a reduction in the average costs of production. In Figure 6-3, as the firm shifts from 10 looms to 20 looms, economies of scale cause average costs to decrease. A doubling of inputs causes output to more than double, making the per unit cost of production decrease.

The LRAC curve slopes upward if diseconomies of scale are dominant. **Diseconomies of scale** (or decreasing returns to scale) occur when an increase in the firm's scale of production causes its average costs of production to increase. In Figure 6-3, as the firm shifts from 20 looms to 30 looms, diseconomies of scale drive up average costs. A doubling of inputs causes output to increase, but not to double, resulting in an increase in the per unit cost of production.

Finally, referring to Figure 6-2, the firm is experiencing constant returns to scale. In this case, a doubling of inputs causes a doubling of output, with no change in the per unit cost of production—the LRAC curve is horizontal.

THINK IT THROUGH: We have not included a long-run marginal cost (LRMC) curve in Figure 6-3 but you should be able to figure out what it must look like, using the average-marginal rule. When the LRAC curve is declining, long-run marginal cost must lie below it—if the cost of extra units is lower than the average, then the average will fall. When long-run average cost is rising, long-run marginal cost must lie above it. Consequently, the LRMC curve must intersect the LRAC curve at the latter's minimum point. Later in this chapter, Figure 6-5 shows the relationship between the two curves.

Causes of Economies of Scale

Economies of scale arise when cost savings occur as the company expands production. Possible sources of economies include the ability of larger firms to adopt technology that would be high cost at low levels of production, negotiate preferential deals with suppliers, gain concessions from politicians, hire personnel to fulfill specialized management function, and so on.

Examples: In the field of electricity generation, the use of larger generators reduces the average cost of production. In banking, where the number of banks has halved in 20 years, the trend toward a smaller number of bigger banks is driven largely by the cost savings involved in such consolidation. Larger farms are more cost-effective than are smaller farms, leading to the expansion of agribusiness and the decline of the family farm. Over the past 70 years, average farm size has tripled and the number of farms has shrunk by two-thirds.

Walmart's dominance in the marketplace is due in part to its powerful negotiating position with its suppliers, many of whom rely on Walmart for most of their sales. Walmart negotiated a deal with Vlasic Pickles to market Vlasic's 3-gallon jar of pickles for $2.97, earning Vlasic a few cents per jar. Shoppers bought the low-priced pickles and stopped buying Vlasic's other, profitable, products. Faced with the threat that Walmart would stop carrying any Vlasic products if the company backed out of the deal, Vlasic filed for bankruptcy in 2001.

THINK IT THROUGH: Can you spot other examples of economies of scale, where bigger means cheaper?

Causes of Diseconomies of Scale

The major source of diseconomies of scale is a breakdown in coordination and communication between departments as the company expands. Failure to communicate effectively may lead to expensive errors. Steve Jobs recognized this problem and placed a limit of 100 persons on his development teams. Other potential problems caused by a firm's unwieldy size include lack of responsiveness to new market challenges or technologies, worker shirking or alienation, lack of morale or effort, and more militant union activity. Finally, government regulations (such as fire, health, or safety regulations) may apply to larger firms but may not apply to smaller firms.

Economies of Scale and the Structure of the Industry

Sometimes, big is not better and small is not beautiful. If there are few economies of scale, the least-cost output level will be achieved at a comparatively low level of production and small firms will dominate. If, however, economies of scale are substantial, the LRAC curve will continue to decline over a wide range of output levels and large firms will have the advantage. If economies dominate diseconomies strongly enough, then the LRAC curve would decline continually.

Industries typified by many small firms—hairdressers, tanning salons, veterinarians, law firms—are likely to experience few economies of scale, whereas industries populated by a few, large, firms—power companies, automobile manufacturers, steel producers—probably have significant economies of scale. Where only one producer monopolizes the market, the presence of a continually downward sloping LRAC curve might be the reason.

Comment: The economies and diseconomies of scale referred to in this section are formally known as *internal economies and diseconomies of scale*—costs change in response to conditions internal to the firm as it expands. There are also *external economies and diseconomies of scale* that affect the firm's costs, not because of a change in its output level but because of external factors, such as the size of the industry itself. The increasing number of high-tech firms in Silicon Valley may have reduced the costs for all of them. Such external economies and diseconomies of scale are beyond the scope of this book.

Long-Run Equilibrium Mechanism: Reaching Balance

In Chapter 5 we concluded that the perfectly competitive firm in the short-run equilibrium might earn an economic profit or loss, or break even. Is this also true in long-run equilibrium? Moreover, how is long-run equilibrium achieved and what conditions hold when it is achieved?

Short-Run Adjustment

When we considered long-run costs, we focused initially on the behavior of short-run costs. Similarly, when looking at the firm's (and market's) adjustment to achieve long-run equilibrium, we begin by considering the short-run environment. We know that the firm may find itself faced with any one of four distinct short-run cases but, for ease of explanation, we

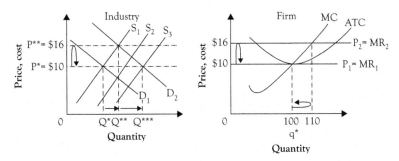

Figure 6-4. The long-run adjustment process.

will assume that the firm is initially "breaking even." The other three cases would give us the same conclusions, but the diagrams and explanations are more elaborate.

Figure 6-4 depicts the demand and supply conditions in an industry in the left panel and a typical individual firm's short-run cost and revenue picture in the right panel.

The industry is at equilibrium where the demand curve (D_1) and supply curve (S_1) intersect. The equilibrium price (P^*) is $10 and the equilibrium quantity (Q^*) is one million units. Given the market price, the firm is maximizing profits by producing at the output level at which marginal revenue equals marginal cost—100 units of output. At this output level, price equals average total cost, therefore the firm is earning zero economic zero economic profit breaking even or earning a normal profit, in other words. This output level for the typical firm implies that there are 10,000 firms, given that the industry's output is a million units.

In this initial situation, because a reasonable rate of return is being earned, there is no incentive for existing firms to leave the industry and no incentive for new firms to enter the industry.

THINK IT THROUGH: In terms of opportunity cost, what does it mean to know that a normal profit is being earned in this industry? When a normal profit is being earned, it means that the reward received by firms in this industry is just sufficient to keep entrepreneurs engaged because it is equal to the reward that can be earned in the best alternative activity. If it were less, then the reward elsewhere would be superior and entrepreneurs would wish to move to the superior reward; if it were more, then the reward in the present industry would exceed the best alternative, and entrepreneurs would wish to enter this industry.

A shock strikes the industry and demand increases from D_1 to D_2— perhaps income level has increased and this is a normal good, or the price of a substitute increased. At the original price level of $10, an industry-wide shortage is now present and the price of the product increases, rising to the new equilibrium level (P^{**}) of $16. The industry's equilibrium output is Q^{**}. Considering the supply curve S_1, there has been an increase in quantity supplied along the curve—a change in price does not change the position of the supply curve.

The price received by the firm has increased, and the profit-maximizing output has risen from 100 units to, say, 110 units—implying that the industry's output level (Q^{**}) is 1.1 million units (110 units × 10,000 firms). The firm is now earning a positive economic profit. This completes the short-run adjustment to the demand shock.

THINK IT THROUGH: We know that the firm's short-run supply curve is, by and large, its marginal cost curve. The increase in price prompts the firm to move along its marginal cost curve—an increase in quantity supplied consistent with the industry-wide increase in quantity supplied.

Comment: While studying Figure 6-4, you may have noticed that quantities for the industry are shown as upper-case (Q), whereas those for the firm are shown as lower-case (q). It is a standard convention in economics to distinguish between industry and firm variables in this manner.

Long-Run Adjustment

At the completion of the short-run adjustment, the typical firm is earning an economic profit. Entrepreneurs outside this industry will be hungry to enter—attracted by the fat pickings available—but, in the short run, entry is not possible and the firms currently present in the industry receive a windfall. However, in the long run, it is possible to enter (or leave) an industry and, drawn by the higher than normal profits, new firms will set up operations and, with free (costless) entry into the market, this process should be rapid.

As new firms enter the industry, the market supply curve will shift to the right, from S_1 to S_2. The market supply curve is the aggregation of the individual firms' supply curves and with more firms, greater supply. Price declines from $16 and, because economic profit is reduced but is still present, there remains an incentive for additional firms to enter the market. As they do so, the market supply curve shifts farther to the right to S_3, further driving down the price and eroding economic profit. When the supply curve reaches S_3, all economic profit has been competed away. Were the supply curve to move farther to the right, then price would be driven down so far that economic losses would be suffered and firms would leave the industry, which, in turn, would pull the supply curve back to the left.

Incentives exist for firms to enter or leave the industry when the supply curve is at any position other than S_3. At S_3, there is no incentive for firms to enter or leave the industry and the market has achieved long-run equilibrium. The final equilibrium price is $10 and the typical firm will produce 100 units of output. The industry's equilibrium quantity (Q^{***}) is 1.2 million units, implying that the number of firms has increased to 12,000.

THINK IT THROUGH: Redo this adjustment process, beginning with a decrease in demand instead of an increase.

Long-Run Equilibrium

In long-run equilibrium, it must be the case that the typical firm earns only a normal profit. Also, the market price must stabilize at the minimum point on the LRAC curve, as shown in Figure 6-5. At any other price profit opportunities would persist, which, in long-run equilibrium, is impossible.

Figure 6-5 includes the LRMC curve. The profit-maximizing condition in long-run equilibrium is that the equilibrium price (marginal

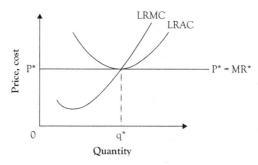

Figure 6-5. The equilibrium relationship between price and the LRAC curve.

revenue) must equal long-run marginal cost at the minimum point on the long-run average cost curve.

P* = MR = LRMC = LRAC (at its minimum value)

When we began our analysis, a particular short-run ATC curve was chosen for Figure 6-4—the one at the minimum point of the LRAC curve, as now shown in Figure 6-6. Any short-run ATC curve could have been chosen as the starting point, but, since competitive pressures must force the price to the minimum point on the LRAC curve, the relevant final short-run ATC curve is the one at the minimum point on the LRAC curve.

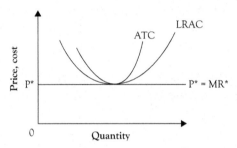

Figure 6-6. The equilibrium relationship between the short-run ATC curve and the LRAC curve.

When the firm is in long-run equilibrium, it earns a normal profit in the long run *and* also in the short run—because, at q*, the price is equal to short-run average total cost. If short-run profits or losses are present, then the industry cannot be in long-run equilibrium.

Notice that, in equilibrium, each firm is forced to produce at the lowest possible cost per unit both in the short run and in the long run in order to survive. Because of free entry into and exit from the market, any firm failing to produce at the most cost-efficient output level will be undercut and eliminated.

THINK IT THROUGH: In Chapter 2, when looking at shifts in demand or supply, we devised a rule—"One factor shifts one curve and it shifts it only one time." Clearly, that rule only applies in the short run. Here, in the long run, a shift in the demand curve prompted a consequent shift in the supply curve. We didn't know it then, but our analysis in Chapter 2 was short run in nature.

The Allocative Role of Economic Profit

In long-run equilibrium, the firm must earn only normal profits, both in the long run and in the short run. What, then, is the role of economic profit? Economic profit operates as a signaling mechanism for producers, indicating where society wishes more of its limited resources to be allocated (the presence of economic profit) and where resource usage should be reduced (the presence of economic losses).

Ethanol: In recent years, American production of corn-based ethanol has been increasing as a substitute for gasoline. The increase in demand for ethanol, with the associated increase in profit, has made corn more profitable for farmers to produce, leading them to plant more acreage in corn and less acreage in wheat. This reallocation of resources has been brought about by changes in the relative profitability of corn and wheat, which, in turn, reflect the relative preferences of consumers.

Henry Ford and the Quadricycle: Ford's first essay into motor vehicles was the "quadricycle," which was powered by ethanol. The time, however, was not ripe for ethanol- or electric-powered vehicles. However, in the past few years, because of the rising price of imported oil and increased "green" awareness, consumers have embraced both the production of ethanol and the development of electric-powered vehicles.

Hydrogen Fuel Cells: In 2008, Honda introduced the FCX Clarity, the first hydrogen fuel cell vehicle. With the increasing demand for this and other nongasoline vehicles (a change in consumer preferences), we would expect the demand for conventional gas-fueled cars to decrease and their profitability to decline, encouraging a transfer of resources toward alternative energy sources.

Shale and Silver: Production and innovation may be stimulated by supply conditions. With declining traditional sources of oil and rising prices, shale oil has become profitable where previously it was not. Similarly, high silver prices have meant that long-closed silver mines once again have become viable profit opportunities and have been reopened.

In each of the examples given here, the self-interested quest for profit was the spark that ignited the reallocation of resources. What other examples can you recall of profitability driving the pattern of resource allocation within the economy?

Efficiency: The Invisible Hand in Motion

We are now in a position to construct criteria to assess the performance of an industry in long-run equilibrium from society's point of view. There are three criteria: whether or not the firm earns normal profits; whether or not it is productively efficient; and whether or not it is allocatively efficient. We will see that perfectly competitive industries satisfy all three of these criteria.

Criterion 1: Normal Profit

Although other goals, such as growth, satisficing, or personal satisfaction, may intervene, the basic assumption in economics is that the entrepreneur is in business to maximize profits. From his or her viewpoint, the more profits earned, the more successful the venture. Society's viewpoint differs. Society wishes to receive the efforts of the entrepreneur at the lowest cost to its customers. A firm earning greater rewards than would be required to maintain the firm in operation is extracting payments from its customers over and above what is necessary. In some sense, such a firm is imposing a private tax on its customers and causing a redistribution of spending power away from the customers and toward the owners of the firm.

These rewards that are "required to maintain the firm in operation" are normal profits. Any additional profits earned by the firm reduce the benefits received by consumers. Our criterion will be to inquire if the typical firm in long-run equilibrium is faced with a price equal to long-run average cost. If it is, then it will fulfill the criterion, but, if not, it will fail to satisfy the criterion. If, in long-run equilibrium, a firm is somehow able to sustain perpetual economic profits, we will see this as a failure from the viewpoint of society.

In long-run equilibrium, we have found that the perfectly competitive firm does earn only a normal profit and, therefore, satisfies this criterion.

Criterion 2: Productive Efficiency, where P = Minimum LRAC

Given its chosen output level, is the firm using the least-cost scale of production and mix of inputs? If it is, then it is achieving productive efficiency; if it is not, then it is falling short and squandering scarce resources.

In Chapter 1, we defined productive efficiency in terms of the production possibility frontier. In that context, the producer is productively efficient if he is on the production possibility frontier as this requires that he is fully employing his resources and using the most effective technology. In the current context, the firm is productively efficient if, given the output level, costs are minimized. Recall that these are opportunity costs—the productively efficient firm is depriving society of the least possible amount of alternatives.

Our criterion for productive efficiency is to determine whether or not the firm is producing at the minimum point on the LRAC curve. In perfect competition, any firm that fails to avail itself of the cheapest, most effective, method of production will be priced out of the market by its rivals.

Criterion 3: Allocative Efficiency, where P (MB) = LRMC

One way to assess an economy's performance is in terms of how well it meets the needs of its consumers. The concept of allocative efficiency captures this notion. An economy has achieved allocative efficiency (also known as Pareto efficiency) if it produces, as cheaply as possible, the commodities that society desires the most. Productive efficiency is a necessary, but not a sufficient, condition. Italian economist Vilfredo Pareto argued that a change is efficient if at least one person is made better off and no person is made worse off as a consequence of that change. If a change hurts some individuals, it is still potentially efficient if the gains outweigh the losses because gainers could fully compensate losers and still come out ahead. An allocatively efficient economy is one in which all such changes have already been made.

THINK IT THROUGH: If you "friend" an additional person on Facebook, or have a colleague become a "connection" in your LinkedIn account, then presumably that person gains from the inclusion and no one loses—this change is Pareto-efficient and should take place.

Our measure of allocative efficiency is to check and see, at the chosen output level, if price equals long-run marginal cost. Recall that price reflects marginal benefit. To produce the "right" output level, the firm (and industry) must expand production if marginal benefit exceeds marginal cost and must reduce output level if marginal cost exceeds marginal benefit. At the P = LRMC output level, no further Pareto-efficient adjustments can be made.

Efficiency, Graphically: Graphically, a market is as efficient as possible when the aggregate of producer surplus and consumer surplus is maximized. Maximum allocative efficiency occurs where the demand curve and supply curve intersect—the total "gain" to society is maximized at equilibrium (Q*), as shown in Figure 6-7.

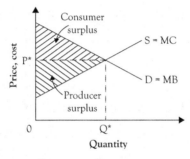

Figure 6-7. Maximum allocative efficiency.

Summary: The major point to take away from this section is that perfectly competitive markets result in maximum allocative efficiency—the "best" mix of outputs, produced as cheaply as possible. As we shall see, any movement away from the perfectly competitive ideal (externalities, for example) leads to distortions—either too much or too little of a good is produced, or the price or cost is too high—and market efficiency is threatened.

Market Failures: Imperfect Results from Perfect Competition

In the preceding sections we have seen that perfect competition yields "good" results—a reasonable rate of return, productive efficiency, and allocative efficiency. These results stem from the conditions of the perfectly competitive model. If any of those assumptions are infringed, then the market may fail to achieve the most socially desirable (optimal) results.

Such suboptimal outcomes are termed market failures. If, for example, entry into an industry can be restricted in such a way that only one firm is present, then that monopoly may be able to extract higher than normal profits and restrict output. Other market failures may occur, however, even if all our stated conditions of perfect competition are met. If, for instance, third parties are affected, positively or negatively, by the production or consumption of a perfectly competitive good, then the market outcome is inefficient—this situation is known as an externality. In this section we consider some important market failures—this topic will be dealt with more fully in Chapter 9.

Some Minor Failures

If all the conditions of perfect competition hold, we may still find results that may be felt to be undesirable. If, for instance, resource markets work perfectly, and owners of resources are rewarded according to the fair value of their contributions to production, then the resulting distribution of spending power may be deemed unfortunate, with the poorly skilled or handicapped receiving particularly low incomes. Society may wish to intervene to "correct" the imbalances in income distribution caused by the operation of the market.

In the relentless drive to reduce costs in the perfectly competitive environment, choice and variety may be sacrificed. Perfect competition assumes a homogeneous product, but consumers may wish for choices of style, color, or location. "One size fits all" may be efficient, but unappealing.

THINK IT THROUGH: Henry Ford famously remarked that buyers of his cars could have any color of vehicle "as long as it's black." Changing paint colors added to costs. Black was chosen as the preferred color because of its rapid drying time (which reduced the likelihood of imperfections). Consumer satisfaction was sacrificed to reduce production costs.

Given that firms will earn no more than a normal profit in long-run equilibrium and are unable to restrict competition through patents, the individual entrepreneur may have little incentive and few funds available for research and development of new products and processes. We might therefore expect low rates of innovation in a perfectly competitive world.

We assumed that buyers and sellers had adequate information when determining what to buy and sell, but this may not be the case. Participants may have *asymmetrical information*. A buyer may be more willing to enter into a contract, such as an insurance policy, if he knows that he is likely to need the coverage. This is known as *adverse selection*. An unhealthy individual is more likely than a healthy one to seek health insurance. Insurance policies have clauses on "preexisting conditions" precisely because of adverse selection.

After the contact has been agreed, *moral hazard* occurs if one of the parties thereafter adjusts their behavior in a way that could be costly to another. Insurance is often given as an example. If a homeowner's insurance covers fire damage, then the homeowner may be less prudent in installing and checking his fire alarms, for instance, thus imposing costs on the insurance firm.

THINK IT THROUGH: Can you think of other ways that insurance firms have written policies to attempt to discourage adverse selection and moral hazard?

THINK IT THROUGH: The effects of seat belts and airbags in cars have been presented as an example of moral hazard. To be sure, such safety devices may reduce the numbers of fatalities for those who wear seat belts or whose cars are equipped with airbags, but evidence suggests that drivers who feel more protected drive more recklessly.

THINK IT THROUGH MORE: During the financial crisis in 2008–2010, some institutions were labeled "too big to fail." Can you see how a belief by the bankers themselves that they were, indeed, "too big to fail" might have encouraged them to indulge in the risky behavior that exacerbated the crisis?

Adverse selection and moral hazard typically spring from buyers having more knowledge than sellers, but preferential knowledge of sellers can also cause markets to fail. In the market for used cars, because the seller typically has greater knowledge than the buyer, the buyer runs the risk of buying a "lemon."

THINK IT THROUGH: The reason that "anti-lemon" laws have been enacted is because asymmetrical information damages the efficient operation of markets.

A Major Market Failure: Externalities

When we drew our demand (marginal benefit) and supply (marginal cost) curves in Figure 6-7, and concluded that producing at the output level where marginal benefit and marginal cost were equal would maximize allocative efficiency, we made an important assumption. We assumed that purchasers of the good were receiving all of the benefits from the consumption of the good and that the producers of the good were bearing all of the costs of its production. In other words, we assumed that all of the benefits and costs flowing from the production and consumption of the good were fully represented in the diagram. But is this always true? In the case of goods exhibiting externalities, it is not. An **externality** occurs when the act of producing or consuming a good creates either external costs or external benefits for third parties who are not involved in the original market transaction.

THINK IT THROUGH: Passive smoking is an example of a cost imposed on third parties who neither produce nor purchase cigarettes as are most forms of pollution. The dangerous activities of a drunk driver or the recklessness of a driver who is chatting on a cell phone or texting are other examples.

Another Major Market Failure: Public Goods

If you buy an apple, then you can retain all of the benefits of the purchase for yourself. You may choose to share, but you don't have to. Similarly, you may lend your pick-up truck to a neighbor who needs to move some furniture, but, again, you may refuse to share your truck. Private goods such as these have a quality of "excludability" that is not present with **public goods**—the purchaser can exclude others from receiving any benefits from his or her purchase if she so wishes. Public goods lack this quality of excludability. A lighthouse is the classic example of a public good. Once the lighthouse is in operation, it is very difficult for the owners of the lighthouse to prevent any passing craft from using the light. If the recipient of the service cannot be easily excluded from receiving the benefits, even if he refuses to pay, then the ability of the firm to generate revenue and to survive is jeopardized. In such a scenario, the private provision of lighthouse services is likely to be inadequate—such public goods may be better provided by society as a whole for society as a whole. We will consider the problems posed by externalities and public goods to the free market system in more detail in Chapter 9.

THINK IT THROUGH: Can you think of other goods or services that bestow benefits that are "nonexcludable" in character? How about public health provision such as flu shots? National defense? Street lighting?

The main conclusion to draw from this section is that even perfectly competitive markets may fail to allocate resources efficiently and to produce the socially optimal mix of goods and services. Because of this, society, in the shape of government laws and regulations, or more direct intervention, may be deemed necessary to compensate for the shortcomings of the market mechanism.

Applications: Nature (and the Market) Abhors a Vacuum

Long-run adjustments in the economy's output mix may be driven by either demand-side or supply-side changes. In all cases, irrational exuberance may lead to the market overshooting—expanding too much too soon—resulting in a compensating contraction. In the extreme case, speculative "bubbles" may develop.

Emus and Ostriches

In 1986, political pressures created a new profit opportunity for American farmers. Health-conscious baby-boomers, who had been seeking alternatives for beef, had discovered that ostrich meat looks and tastes like beef but with far less cholesterol, calories, and fat and the demand for ostrich meat, imported from South Africa, had become established in the United States. The Reagan Administration, after some years of "constructive engagement," bowed to increasingly strident public demands for the imposition of a trade embargo on imported South African products, including ostrich meat. Suddenly, there was a demand without a supply. Some American farmers, attracted by the promise of profits, moved away from the sagging beef industry and toward ostrich and emu production. Emus and ostriches offered a generous return, as the birds can produce meat, eggs, leather, and feathers. In addition, the initial set-up costs of $100,000 were comparatively low. With few barriers to entry, a proven market demand, and limited foreign competition, it was not surprising that the American ostrich market took off.

Because entry into the market was relatively easy, early entrants earned substantial economic profits. However, as new firms entered the industry, the market supply curve shifted to the right, driving down the price. By the late 1990s, prices had tumbled. Furthermore, on the supply side, trade restrictions on South African products were removed leading to increased foreign supply. Only normal profits were being earned in the long run.

At this juncture, emu farming appeared as an alternative for ostriches, with emu meat a healthy alternative for beef, and emu oil and leather as additional revenue streams. In the long run, normal profits only were being earned, with many farmers opting out of the market and releasing their stock.

Note: A similar, politically driven, profit opportunity sprang up in the 1970s, with the Iranian Revolution. Until that time, the bulk of pistachios bought in the United States were produced in Iran. Following the overthrow of the Shah, the United States embargoed the importation of Iranian pistachios and, sensing a profit opportunity, Californian entrepreneurs filled the vacuum establishing an industry where none had been before.

Medical Care and Baby-Boomers

Just as profit opportunities may arise from supply-side changes (new technology or laws, for example) demand-side considerations may be the spur to market adjustments. As the baby-boomers age and retire, the demand will increase for medical services to treat their ailments—more hip replacements, heart operations, and plastic surgery—and for personnel to staff nursing homes. Demographic changes will shape the landscape of the economy, reflecting the evolving preferences of consumers.

Review: If an unfulfilled need is present in the market place, then an opportunity exists to earn profits. The reason entrepreneurs enter the market, hire resources, and set up production is because they detect profit opportunities. The greater the needs of society, the greater the profit opportunities that exist, and the greater will be the allocation of resources to meet those needs.

CHAPTER 7

Monopoly

By the end of this chapter you will be able to:

1. Specify the conditions that may permit the development of a "single-seller" monopoly and, using the two broad types of barriers to entry, identify two types of monopoly.
2. Explain why the monopolist's marginal revenue decreases as output increases.
3. Draw and interpret a diagram representing the price and output choices of a profit-maximizing monopolist.
4. Draw a diagram to compare a monopolist's performance relative to that of a perfectly competitive firm in terms of price, output, and the effect on income distribution.
5. Identify the long-run welfare loss caused by the presence of an "artificial" monopoly and show it graphically.
6. Explain what is meant by price discrimination and discuss its effects.
7. Distinguish a natural monopoly from other forms of monopoly.
8. Identify the two broad policy stances taken by the government with regard to an industry that exhibits monopoly characteristics and the two government organizations charged with combating anticompetitive practices.

Lipitor, the cholesterol-reducing drug, has been the world's best-selling branded medication in pharmaceutical history, topping the sales performance lists since the late 1990s. Pfizer, its developer, has enjoyed a lucrative monopoly, protected by patent law. In May 2012, generic drug makers became able to market their competing versions but it's a safe bet that Lipitor will continue to earn profits for Pfizer, supported by name-brand recognition and advertising. This situation—one seller of a patent-protected product with name-brand recognition—is far from perfect competitive model we have explored in the two previous chapters but it is one that has been created and sustained by our legal system. In this chapter, we consider why.

Chapter Preview: In Chapters 5 and 6 we examined the consequences of having production organized through perfectly competitive industries and discovered that perfect competition gave society generally beneficial results, through the operation of what Adam Smith termed the "invisible hand" of self-interest. However, perfect competition is a rare beast in the real world and, in this chapter, we turn our attention to the other end of the competitive spectrum—monopoly, the market structure in which one firm dominates the industry.

Brain Teaser: Monopoly has frequently received a bad press and, certainly, our conclusions in Chapter 6 would seem to argue that perfect competition bestows beneficial results in terms of productive efficiency and allocative efficiency. Can you think of any examples or circumstances where we would prefer to have a single producer instead of perfect competition?

The Making and Maintenance of a Monopoly: Is One the Loneliest Number?

Characteristics of a Monopoly

A **pure monopoly** arises when there is a single firm in an industry producing a good or service with no close substitutes and where there are significant barriers to the entry of competitors. Clearly, the trick is to define what comprises the relevant market. There is a market for Budweiser beer, but Budweiser is not a monopoly because there are other brands of beer available that, for most buyers, are sufficiently similar. However, Microsoft's bundling its own browser and other products with its Windows operating system was found by the courts to be the practice of an "abusive" monopoly. Note that a monopoly need not be a large nationwide firm— your local water and sewage provider is likely to be a monopolist, as is your local cable TV provider.

Whereas the perfectly competitive firm is a "price taker" (having no independent control over the price of his product), the monopolist is said to be a "price maker." The monopolist *is* the industry and can choose to set any price he desires, although we continue to assume his actions are guided by the goal of profit-maximization. It is because of this power to dictate price that many monopolies are subject to government regulation.

Initially, we assume that the firm sets the same price for all customers, but, in many instances, monopolists practice **price discrimination**— setting different prices for different classes of customer. We look at the implications of price discrimination later in this chapter.

Circumstances may create a situation where there is only one seller of a good—a tornado rips through town, destroying all the stores but one—but usually we think of a monopoly as having more staying power than this. For a monopoly to develop and endure, there must exist some sort of restriction that prevents competitors from entering and competing with the monopolist. These restrictions are known as **barriers to entry**.

Barriers to Entry

Artificial Barriers to Entry

Barriers to entry may be "artificial" or "natural." An **artificial barrier to entry**, which often is legal in nature, imposes an artificial restriction on competition—"artificial" in the sense that the barrier exists simply because society has chosen to impose it. For example, patent laws bestow monopoly power on firms—Pfizer's right to be the sole producer of Lipitor is due to patent laws; if these laws were modified, then the legal basis for such monopolists would vanish.

Other artificial barriers to entry include government licenses, franchise agreements, ownership or control of key resources, and overpowering advertising budgets or name identification with a class of product.

THINK IT THROUGH. Can you think of real-world examples of monopolies (or near-monopolies) sustained by each of these barriers? Cable TV companies have monopoly power due to government licenses; marketing of foreign products can be encouraged through franchise agreements; Alcoa once had a stranglehold on aluminum production because of its ownership of bauxite mines; and Coke, Kleenex, and Xerox all have had advantages over would-be rivals because of name recognition.

There may be good economic reasons for the establishment of an "artificial" monopoly. Having only one firm operating in an area may prevent wasteful duplication of service or underemployment of resources—it makes little sense to have two or more sets of water lines in a neighborhood, for example. The profit-earning attraction of a new process or product may stimulate creativity if the innovation can be protected by patent while exclusive marketing rights may encourage the provision of a new good or service that might otherwise not be offered to customers. After all, why go to the expense of researching and developing a new product, then educating consumers about its advantages, if a low-cost competitor is then allowed to come into the market and undercut the original developer's price?

Natural Barriers to Entry

A **natural barrier to entry** is one that occurs through the nature of the market itself and results in the development of a **natural monopoly**. The most obvious example of this type of barrier is the presence of substantial economies of scale. As we saw in Chapter 6, as a firm expands its scale of operations, economies of scale drive down the per-unit cost of production.

Suppose we have 20 companies in competition, with each firm producing 100 units of output at an average cost of $10. Total industry production is 2000 units. The long-run average cost (LRAC) curve for each firm is identical and shown in Figure 7-1.

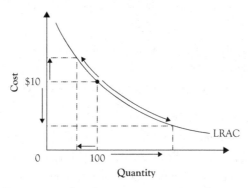

Figure 7-1. Economies of scale creating a monopoly.

The continually downward-sloping appearance of the LRAC curve tells us that ongoing economies of scale are present. This is a potentially unstable situation because if one firm (Firm A) attracts a few customers from each of its rivals, then the market will evolve into a monopoly. As Firm A's output expands, its average costs decrease and it will be able to reduce its price, whereas Firm A's rivals will service fewer customers and, with lower output and rising average costs, will increase price. Firm A's relatively cheaper price will attract more customers to switch from its rivals—its output will expand further and its price will decrease more, while the output of its rivals will contract further, forcing them to raise prices again. Assuming that Firm A's economies of scale are sufficiently sustained to service the entire market, the culmination of the process will be a monopoly—a natural monopoly.

Note that there is no mechanism present to encourage renewed competition. Any new firm entering the market, with a small scale of production and the associated high costs, would be forced out by low-cost, low-price Firm A.

We would expect to see a natural monopoly in an industry with substantial economies of scale, or in one that has high set-up costs (electricity generation, for example).

Other situations where it is "natural" to have a single firm will be dealt with more fully in the section on natural monopolies.

Monopoly in the Short Run: Stellio's Pizzeria

In this section we consider the behavior of the "artificial" monopolist in the short run and, in the following section, the long-run implications. After that, we turn to the special aspects of natural monopoly.

Monopolies need not be large national firms—many monopolies thrive in local markets. The benign country store in the small rural town may, in many respects, be a monopolist and, in our example, so is Stellio's Pizzeria and Fish Restaurant. Stellio runs his pizzeria in a small, fairly isolated town and his is the only restaurant for many miles. If you crave a restaurant meal, then it has to be served at Stellio's. Stellio's monopoly is sustained not by a legal barrier to entry but, in fact, by an illegal one. He has Mafia connections and restaurateurs who have set up

in opposition to Stellio in the past have had a nasty history of unfortunate "accidents."

The Monopolist's Revenue Picture

We can set up a demand schedule for Stellio's pizzas. The law of demand
would have us expect that higher prices would lead to fewer pizzas being
demanded each hour and this pattern is shown in Table 7-1.

Table 7-1. Revenue Information for Stellio's Pizzeria

Price of a Pizza	Quantity of Pizzas Demanded	Total Revenue	Marginal Revenue
$13	0	0	
$12	1	$12	$12
$11	2	$22	$10
$10	3	$30	$8
$9	4	$36	$6
$8	5	$40	$4
$7	6	$42	$2

If Stellio increases the price of his pizzas, then quantity demanded will
decrease—the law of demand holds true just as firmly in the monopoly
market as it does in perfect competition.

Total revenue (TR) or total spending was introduced in Chapter 4,
and defined as price times quantity demanded (P × q). This definition also
holds for the monopolist and we use it to complete the "total revenue"
column in the table.

THINK IT THROUGH: Table 7-1 has no column for average revenue, but do
we need a separate column for average revenue? Average revenue (AR)
was defined in Chapter 5 as total revenue divided by quantity and, we
saw at that time, it is simply another name for price. When price is $9,
total revenue is $36, quantity is 4, and average revenue is $9 (the same
as price).

Marginal revenue (MR) was defined in Chapter 5 as how much total
revenue changes as an extra unit is sold.

$$MR = \Delta TR/\ \Delta q$$

Again, we can apply that definition to determine the extra revenue brought in from each additional pizza sold. If Stellio charges $11 per pizza, then his total revenue is $22. If he cuts his price to $10, then he sells another pizza and his total revenue increases to $30.

$$MR = \Delta TR/\Delta q = +\$8/+1 = \$8$$

We can complete the "marginal revenue" column in Table 7-1.

THINK IT THROUGH: Note that marginal revenue is positive decreasing as additional pizzas are sold. Can marginal revenue fall so low that it becomes zero, or even negative? Yes, marginal revenue can become zero or negative. This is related to the Total Revenue Test of elasticity in Chapter 4. When price decreases, we know that quantity demanded increases—in terms of the marginal revenue formula, Δq is positive. However, the effect on the numerator of the formula (ΔTR) depends on elasticity. If demand is elastic, then a price decrease will cause total revenue to increase (ΔTR is positive), and marginal revenue will be a positive value. If, however, demand is inelastic, then a price decrease will cause total revenue to decrease (ΔTR is negative), and marginal revenue will be a negative value. Finally, if demand is unit-elastic, then a price decrease will have no effect on total revenue (ΔTR is zero), and marginal revenue will be zero.

When we looked at the perfectly competitive firm, we derived its "revenue picture" and found that it was a single horizontal line. The monopolist's revenue picture is a bit more complicated. Stellio's revenue picture is shown in Figure 7-2.

The revenue picture for a monopolist features a downward-sloping industry demand curve—which also represents price (P), average revenue (AR), and marginal benefit (MB)—and a downward-sloping marginal revenue (MR) curve.

THINK IT THROUGH: The relationship between these two curves harks back to the "average-marginal rule" that we developed in Chapter 5.

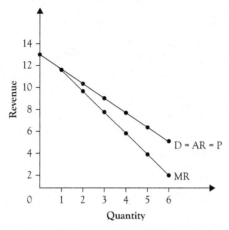

Figure 7-2. The monopolist's revenue picture.

First, we know that marginal revenue must lie below average revenue. Why? Because average revenue is decreasing. We also know that the two curves must start at the same point—for the first observation, the average and marginal values are equal. We saw this same phenomenon when we looked at the relationship between average product and marginal product and, again, when we looked at the relationship between average variable cost and marginal cost. If you're unsure about the previous statements, go back now and revisit the average-marginal rule.

Comment for the mathematically minded reader: The MR curve is twice as steep as the AR curve.

The Monopolist's Short-Run Cost Picture

Just as we have developed a revenue picture for the firm, so we can derive its short-run cost picture. In fact, there is no new work to be done here because the cost picture for the monopolist is identical to that of the perfectly competitive firm. Why? Because the monopolist is just as closely governed by the law of diminishing marginal productivity and the interplay of the specialization effect and the congestion effect as the perfectly competitive firm. To be sure, the number of units the monopolist produces may be much larger than that for the perfectly competitive firm, but the principles and the relationship developed in Chapter 5 are the same—nothing new to learn.

Table 7-2 shows Stellio's short-run costs.

Table 7-2. Short-Run Cost Information for Stellio's Pizzeria

Quantity of Pizzas Produced	Total Cost	Marginal Cost
0	$9	
1	$11	$2
2	$14	$3
3	$18	$4
4	$24	$6
5	$32	$8
6	$43	$11

In the short run, the firm has some fixed resource and, therefore, some fixed costs that it incurs even when output is zero—Stellio's total fixed cost (TFC) is $9. Total variable cost (TVC) is zero when no pizzas are produced, but will increase, as will total cost (TC), as pizza production is stepped up, as shown in the table—for instance, when 4 pizzas are produced, total cost is $24, total fixed cost is (still) $9, and total variable cost is $15.

THINK IT THROUGH: What might these fixed resources be? What are Stellio's variable resources?

We are familiar with marginal cost (MC) from Chapter 5. Marginal cost is defined as

$$MC = \Delta TC/\Delta q$$

For instance, as output expands from 4 pizzas to 5 pizzas, total cost increases from $24 to $32, and the marginal cost of the fifth pizza is $8.

The firm's short-run cost picture shown in Figure 7-3, and the production and cost relationships it represents, is indistinguishable from the one derived for perfect competition, that is, Figure 5-11.

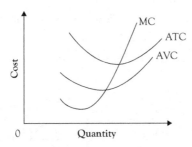

Figure 7-3. The monopolist's short-run cost picture.

Profit Maximization

The monopolist follows the same principles as the perfectly competitive firm when seeking to maximize his profit. As we saw in Figure 5-15 of Chapter 5, there are three possible relationships between price (average revenue) and average total cost (ATC)—the demand curve can intersect, be tangent to, or entirely miss the ATC curve. These relationships are shown in Figure 7-4.

In Case 1, the firm can earn a positive economic profit because, at least at some output levels, its average revenue exceeds its average cost. In Case 2 (the break-even case), the best the firm can manage is zero economic profit—a normal profit is earned. In Cases 3 and 4, the firm will earn a negative economic profit and must decide whether to produce (Case 3) or shut down (Case 4).

We look at each of these cases in turn but the important point to keep in mind is that, although the diagrams may appear more complex, the principles involved for the monopolist are exactly the same as those we developed in Chapter 5 for the perfectly competitive firm.

Comment: Before proceeding, you may wish to review the sections in Chapter 5 on the "Four Short-run Cases" and the "General Procedure for Short-Run Profit Maximization," both of which are highly pertinent here.

Case 1: Positive Economic Profit

When the product's price exceeds average total cost, the firm can earn a positive economic profit. To maximize profit, the firm should produce at the output level (q*) where MR = MC. At this output level, the difference

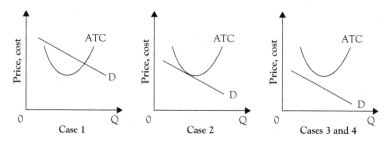

Figure 7-4. Relationships between price and average total cost.

between price and average total cost (P – ATC) represents the economic profit per unit. Multiplying by the number of units gives us the total economic profit.

Table 7-3 provides information for Stellio's Pizzeria.

Table 7-3. Stellio's Pizzeria and Profit Maximization

Quantity of Pizzas	Price	Total Revenue	Total Cost	Marginal Revenue	Marginal Cost	Economic Profit
0	$13	$0	$9		0	–$9
1	$12	$12	$11	$12	$2	$1
2	$11	$22	$14	$10	$3	$8
3	$10	$30	$18	$8	$4	$12
4	$9	$36	$24	$6	$6	$12
5	$8	$40	$32	$4	$8	$8
6	$7	$42	$43	$2	$11	–$1

Comparing the marginal revenue and marginal cost columns, marginal revenue equals marginal cost when 4 pizzas are produced each hour. Accordingly, Stellio should set his price to $9 per pizza to attract the profit-maximizing number of orders. Comparing total revenue ($36) and total cost ($24), we see that his total economic profit is $12 per hour.

We could arrive at the same result using the following alternative method:

$$\text{Total economic profit} = (P - ATC)q^*$$
$$= (\$9.00 - \$6.00)\,4$$
$$= \$12.00$$

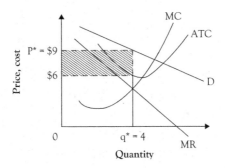

Figure 7-5. Case 1: positive economic profit.

We can depict the same conclusion with Figure 7-5.

If, as is the case in this example, the demand curve intersects the average total cost curve, then a positive economic profit can be earned. To interpret the diagram, recall that the firm's first interest is to determine this profit-maximizing output level (q*). This occurs where marginal revenue and marginal cost are equal (at 4 pizzas). The price associated with this output level is determined by the *demand* curve. Total economic profit is represented by the shaded area in Figure 7-5.

Comment: Many students find it tempting to go to the vertical axis directly from the intersection between marginal revenue and marginal cost. This is wrong, but understandable. In perfect competition, marginal revenue and price were the same value but, in monopoly, a bit more caution is called for.

The remaining three short-run cases are presented briefly—the principles involved are no different from those developed in Chapter 5 for the perfectly competitive firm.

Case 2: Zero Economic Profit—The Break-Even Case

If the demand curve touches the ATC curve at only one point, then this output level must be the profit-maximizing output level (q*)—at every other level of output, an economic loss must be incurred because price (average revenue) is less than average total cost. Accordingly, q* must be the output level at which marginal revenue and marginal cost are equal. The profit-maximizing price is P*. See Figure 7-6.

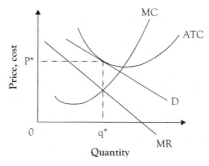

Figure 7-6. Case 2: zero economic profit.

Comment: In all other cases, the downward-sloping marginal revenue curve can be drawn in the short-run monopoly diagram without much caution—as long as the MR curve is drawn below the demand curve then a reasonable diagram should ensue. However, in this case, care must be taken to ensure that the diagram is consistent. The intersection of the MR curve and the MC curve determines the profit-maximizing output level (q*) and this output level *must* be the one at which the demand curve is tangent to the ATC curve. If the diagram is drawn otherwise, then it is inconsistent—you can't have two "best" output levels!

As we saw in perfect competition, the firm earning zero economic profit will continue to produce—the entrepreneur is earning a normal profit (a reasonable rate of return equivalent to his opportunity costs).

Case 3: Negative Economic Profit but Continuing to Produce

When the demand curve lies below the ATC curve at every output level, then the firm must earn a negative economic profit. As with the perfect competitor, the monopolist must decide whether or not to produce. Fortunately, the rule we created when looking at perfect competition is equally applicable for a monopolist—if, at the profit-maximizing (that is, loss-minimizing) output level, the firm's price equals or exceeds its average variable cost, then it should produce, but, if its price is less than its average variable cost, then it should shut down. Figure 7-7 depicts the former case while Figure 7-8 depicts the latter.

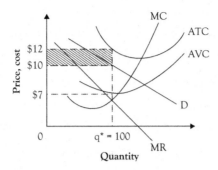

Figure 7-7. Case 3: negative economic profit but continuing to produce.

If this firm should produce at all, then it should produce at q*, where MR = MC. This requires q* to be 100 units of output. At this output, the demand curve dictates a price of $10, but average total cost is greater—say, $12. The firm will suffer a total economic loss of $200.

$$\text{Total economic profit} = (P - ATC)q^*$$
$$= (\$10.00 - \$12.00)\,100$$
$$= -\$200.00$$

Total economic profit (a loss in this case) is represented by the shaded area in Figure 7-7.

Can this firm do better by shutting down? If it does shut down, then its total revenue will be zero and its total cost will be limited to its total fixed cost as the firm can divest itself of its variable resources. Its total economic loss, therefore, will equal its total fixed cost. We can determine the firm's total fixed cost—it is $500.

At q*, ATC is $12. We can see that AVC is $7, meaning that AFC must be $5. Total fixed costs (AFC × q) must therefore be $500.

By producing, the firm loses $200; by not producing, it loses more—it's better for the firm to suffer the smaller loss and continue to operate.

THINK IT THROUGH: As long as AVC is less than price, then it must be true that the total fixed cost will exceed total economic loss and, therefore, the better option is to stay in business instead of shutting down.

Case 4: Negative Economic Profit—The Shut-Down Case

When the firm's price is so low that it can find no level of production at which it can cover its variable costs, then the firm's best interests are served by shutting down. We can see this in the following example, as shown in Figure 7-8.

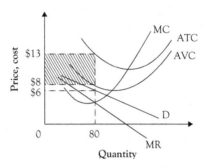

Figure 7-8. Case 4: negative economic profit—the shut-down case.

In this case, the profit-maximizing output level (if the firm opts to produce) is 80 units. This is where MR = MC. On the basis of the demand curve, the price is $6 but the average total cost is $13. If it goes ahead, then the firm will lose $7 on each unit produced, or $560.

If however, the firm shuts down, then its total revenue will be zero and its total cost will be limited to its total fixed cost. Total fixed cost is average fixed cost times the number of units and is constant at all output levels. At 80 units of output, because ATC is $13 and AVC is $8, then AFC must be $5. Total fixed cost must be $400. If the firm shuts down then its loss will be lower than if it produces.

As we saw with perfect competition, the distinction between Case 3 and Case 4 lies in the relationship between price and average variable cost. At any price equal to or above the minimum value for average variable cost, production should proceed because the producer can fully pay the variable resources and may have additional revenues that can defray some of the fixed expenses. If, however, the product's price is less than average variable cost, the firm should cease operations. There is no point hiring resources that can't pay their way.

Profit-Maximizing for the Monopolist

What this sequence of examples has shown is that the short-run profit-maximizing technique for the monopolist is indistinguishable from that of the perfectly competitive firm. Propelled by their own self-interest, they think, and act, alike.

The Monopolist's (Missing) Short-Run Supply Curve

You may recall from Chapter 5 that, after considering the "four short-run cases," we derived the perfectly competitive firm's short-run supply curve and may have an expectation that we will now do the same for the monopolist. However, it is not possible for us to derive a unique "price–quantity supplied" relationship for the monopolist. Figure 7-9 shows the problem.

A supply curve depicts a unique, one-to-one relationship between price and quantity supplied and, in perfect competition, we found that that relationship was governed by marginal cost. No such unique relationship can be derived for the monopolist because demand-side conditions are unpredictable. Let us suppose that the monopolist's demand curve is D_1. Its profit-maximizing output level is q* (where $MR_1 = MC$). However, if the monopolist's demand curve is D_2 then its profit-maximizing output level is still q* (where $MR_2 = MC$). Two prices (P_1 and P_2) but one output level—there is no unique monopoly supply curve.

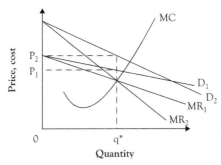

Figure 7-9. The non-unique "price–quantity" relationship.

Monopoly in the Long Run: Long-Run Equilibrium Outcomes in Artificial Monopoly

We are now ready to turn our attention to the behavior of the "artificial" monopoly in the long run and, more particularly, in long-run equilibrium. In a natural monopoly, long-run average cost (LRAC) continues to decline because of substantial economies of scale. This is not true for the artificial monopoly—the LRAC curve is U-shaped.

In Chapter 6, we saw that, in long-run equilibrium, the typical perfectly competitive firm will be driven, by the entry and exit of rivals, to a situation where only a normal profit will be earned. However, in monopoly, there are no rivals and economic profits can be preserved, even in long-run equilibrium.

There are two possible cases. The first, unlikely, but possible, case is that the firm will earn only a normal profit. This outcome *could* occur, but it is important to realize that there is no mechanism in monopoly that would compel it to occur—it just would be the accidental alignment of the demand-side and supply-side conditions. The second, and more likely, case is that the firm will earn economic profits.

Case 1: Long-Run Equilibrium with Zero Economic Profits

We consider the less likely case first, as shown in Figure 7-10.

At first glance, this diagram looks similar to Figure 7-6 and, in one respect, they tell the same story, that the firm is earning only normal

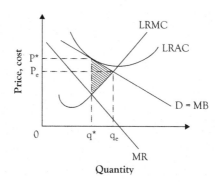

Figure 7-10. Long-run equilibrium with zero economic profits.

profits. Profit maximization occurs at the output level (q*) where the demand curve is tangent to the LRAC curve (and where MR = MC). The firm will charge a price of P*. The important difference is that the current context is long run whereas in Figure 7-6 the context was short run. There is nothing inherent in this market that will cause change—firms cannot enter (and, given that only normal profits are being earned, none will wish to enter) and the firm will remain in business as it is earning a reasonable rate of return.

Performance Criteria—A Review

In Chapter 6, we developed three performance criteria for a firm in long-run equilibrium—that the firm earn only a normal profit; that the firm be productively efficient (producing at the output level where long-run average costs are minimized); and that the firm be allocatively efficient (producing at the output level where price (marginal benefit) equals long-run marginal cost). Perfect competition fulfilled these criteria well—but what about monopoly?

The Monopolist's Performance

We can relate what we learned about economic performance in Chapter 6 to the situation as depicted in Figure 7-10. The monopolist is earning only a normal profit (Criterion 1). However, the monopolist fails the other two tests—the firm is neither productively efficient nor allocatively efficient. The firm is not productively efficient because, at its chosen output level (q*), long-run average costs are still decreasing—it should expand its output. The firm is not allocatively efficient because, at q*, the price that consumers are willing to pay exceeds the long-run marginal cost of production. Again, the firm should expand output, in this instance, to q_e.

Left to its own devices, however, the firm will not expand output—it has achieved its preferred output level at q* and preferred price at P*. If the monopolist were to expand output to the allocatively efficient level, q_e, then, to attract the additional customers, the price of the product would have to decrease to P_e. We can conclude, then, that the profit-maximizing monopolist's self-interest leads him to restrict output to a level that is less than the socially optimal level (q_e), and sets a price to be higher than the socially optimal price (P$_e$). The monopolist imposes a deadweight welfare loss on society equal to the "gap" between marginal benefit (MB) and marginal cost in the range of output denied society from q* to q$_e$, as shown by the shaded area in Figure 7-10.

Case 2: Long-Run Equilibrium with Positive Economic Profits

The more likely situation is that the monopolist will earn positive economic profits, and this case is shown in Figure 7-11.

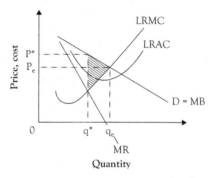

Figure 7-11. Long-run equilibrium with positive economic profits.

The Monopolist's Performance

The story is similar to the previous case. The monopolist will produce q*, where MR = MC, setting a price of P*. Because the price exceeds long-run average cost, the monopolist is earning an economic profit—he fails Criterion 1. The monopolist also fails the other criteria. The firm is not productively efficient (Criterion 2) because, at its chosen output level (q*), long-run average costs are not minimized. The firm is not allocatively efficient (Criterion 3) because, at q*, marginal benefit exceeds marginal cost—the firm should expand output to q$_e$. Society incurs a deadweight welfare loss equal to the "gap" between marginal benefit (MB) and marginal cost, as shown by the shaded area in Figure 7-11.

THINK IT THROUGH: In fact, the firm *could* be productively efficient, but it would be a fluke. If demand conditions were such that the marginal revenue curve passed through the minimum point on the LRAC curve

then the monopolist would choose to produce at the productively efficient output level. Draw it and confirm this!

THINK IT THROUGH MORE: It is impossible for the monopolist to maximize
profits and also achieve allocative efficiency. Profit maximization requires
that MR = MC. Allocative efficiency requires that MB = MC. To accom-
plish both goals would require that MR = MB and, with a downward-
sloping demand curve, we know that marginal revenue will be less than
marginal benefit.

The profit-maximizing monopolist generally fails on each of the three
performance criteria. In contrast, perfectly competitive industries perform well. The monopolist overprices and underproduces, denies consumers the socially optimal output level, squanders resources, and, in the
case of the firm earning economic profits, forces a redistribution of spending power away from the customers and to the owners of the monopoly.
This unflattering scorecard has been the theoretical justification for over a
century of antitrust legislation and regulation of monopoly.

The Case of an Industry where there are no Economies of Scale

In Chapter 6 we determined that the U-shape of the LRAC curve was due
to the presence of economies and diseconomies of scale. Are our conclusions regarding the relative merits of perfect competition and monopoly
affected by the presence or absence of such factors?

Consider Figure 7-12, in which the LRAC curve is horizontal, implying that there are no economies or diseconomies of scale.

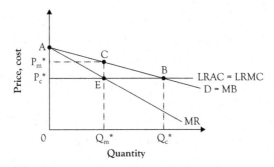

*Figure 7-12. Graphical comparison of perfect competition
and monopoly.*

Initially, let us suppose that we have an industry composed of many perfectly competitive firms. Given that the LRAC curve is horizontal, the average-marginal rule should convince us that the single line also represents long-run marginal cost (LRMC). We have established that, under perfect competition, the industry will expand production until price (or marginal benefit) equals marginal cost. Long-run output is at Q_c^* and the market price is P_c^*. The consumer surplus is P_c^*AB—the area between the marginal benefit curve and the marginal cost curve.

THINK IT THROUGH: Verify that, at Q_c^*, the perfectly competitive industry is meeting each of the three performance criteria.

What will be the effects if the firms are consolidated into one monopoly organization? First, because the firm is now a price maker, we must consider the marginal revenue curve. The profit-maximizing monopolist will set price at P_m^* and output at Q_m^*.

A comment on notation: Throughout this chapter, we have viewed the monopoly as a firm and used lower-case letters in diagrams (e.g., q^*) to be consistent with previous chapters. In this example, because we're making an industry comparison, upper-case letters are being used.

The presence of the monopoly has increased price and decreased output. Productive and allocative efficiency have suffered. The consumer surplus that was being received under perfect competition has shrunk to P_m^*AC—consumers have lost ground. Part of the original consumer surplus has been appropriated by the monopolist as economic profits. Recalling that P_c^* represents the firm's average cost and P_m represents its price, the monopoly is earning an economic profit shown by the area $P_c^* P_m^*CE$—income distribution has shifted in favor of the owners of the monopoly. The remaining portion of P_c^*AB—the triangle CEB—represents the deadweight welfare loss caused to society by the presence of the monopolist.

Because of the deleterious effects of monopolies (and other forms of imperfect competition), the government may choose to intervene to improve the allocation of society's resources. There are two apparently conflicting government positions—first, promotion of competition and restriction of market power through trust-busting legislation and, second, restriction of competition by regulation of industries. Antitrust actions are meant to promote competition; regulation intends to restrict competition. Both policies are intended to promote allocative efficiency.

Antitrust actions prevent monopolies from forming or, if they have formed, break them up or inject additional competitive elements into the market. In banking, for instance, economies of scale favor larger banks and, therefore, regulations have been established to enhance the viability of smaller banks. A similar statement could be made about family farms. The Antitrust Division of the Department of Justice enforces antitrust laws and must approve mergers between firms and it may refuse if the merger is felt not to be in the public interest. The Federal Trade Commission was also created to investigate unfair competition. The courts can impose civil and criminal penalties and can specifically forbid illegal actions in the future.

The Sherman Act of 1890 made monopoly and trade restraints illegal. Subsequent legislation has made it clear that the key issue is not whether a firm is a monopoly but whether its actions to establish and secure its position represent "unreasonable conduct."

Think about an opposite case: Currently, there are 18 alcoholic beverage control (ABC) states. Although the particular controls vary from state to state, the common feature is that the sale of liquor is regulated by a monopoly organization run by the state government. We can predict the effect of such a monopoly presence in the market—the price of alcohol will be higher and sales will be lower. Indeed, ABC regulations were frequently promoted by temperance organizations that wished for precisely such an outcome!

Price Discrimination

So far, we have assumed that the firm charges all customers the same price but the monopolist may be able to practice price discrimination, where the same product is sold at different prices to different consumers. For price discrimination to be effective, the firm must be able to identify who will be willing to pay the higher price and must be able to prevent resale.

THINK IT THROUGH: Price discrimination surrounds us, although usually it's expressed as special discounted prices for select customers, not special high prices for some customers. Senior citizen or student discounts, frequent flier bonuses, and differential rates for children in movies or restaurants are all examples, as are quantity discounts such as "buy one, get one free." The friendly car saleswoman is intently trying to assess her customer's willingness to pay for the new car he's interested in buying. In recent years, soft drinks machines have adjusted prices according to the temperature—higher temperature, higher price. Airlines offering the same seat to different customers, or hotels offering the same room to different guests, but charging different prices are practicing price discrimination. A student receiving financial aid, or one who pays "in-state" tuition, is deriving benefits from price discrimination whereas nonrecipients and out-of-state students are penalized.

Perfect price discrimination occurs when the firm is able to charge each customer the maximum amount that that customer is willing to pay. The price charged equals the customer's marginal benefit and the entire consumer surplus is appropriated by the producer. In such a situation, the extra revenue derived from the sale of an additional unit of output is equal to the price charged to the customer. In other words, marginal revenue and price are equal. Graphically, the firm's demand curve is also its marginal revenue curve.

Armed with this new information, let's revisit Figure 7-12. If the firm is able to price discriminate perfectly, then the original marginal revenue disappears and the demand curve represents marginal revenue. The profit-maximizing monopolist will produce at the output level where marginal revenue equals marginal cost, namely Q_c^*, the allocatively efficient output level. Price discrimination can correct a misallocation of resources.

THINK IT THROUGH: The entire area P_c^*AB will be taken over as profits by the monopolist! Can you see why?

Natural Monopoly: Regulation of Monopoly

As we have seen, some monopolies are the natural product of market forces. Such "natural" monopolies are often due to the existence of substantial economies of scale or extremely high set-up costs. The presence of network externalities is another reason why a single firm might be the most desirable market structure. Network externalities arise when the value of a good or service to a customer increases as the number of users increase—having one firm such as eBay is more beneficial for customers than spreading auctions over many small firms.

THINK IT THROUGH: It makes sense to have one social media provider—Facebook has thrived while MySpace has withered. One service location adds value for the customer. Similarly, software and Internet services, including interactive video games, are more valuable for all users the more subscribers are added into the system. My purchase of a cell phone bestows benefits not only for me but also for those who wish to phone me.

THINK IT THROUGH: Before the events of 9/11, airport security was provided by privately contracted firms. Following 9/11, many of these firms were felt to be inadequate and the Transportation Security Administration (TSA) was set up. The belief was that an integrated government monopoly would perform more effectively than a patchwork of private firms. One option, then, is that the government can wholly take over and manage an industry, such as airport security or the post office, but this course of action is infrequently pursued in the United States.

When a natural monopoly is present, we would wish to preserve the benefits bestowed by the monopoly, but to regulate it. We can see the theory underlying regulation in Figure 7-13. Let us assume that the firm is an electric company—Sparx.

The diagram signals that Sparx is a natural monopoly because the LRAC curve is continually downward-sloping. Left to itself, the profit-maximizing firm will set price (P*) and output (q*) based on the

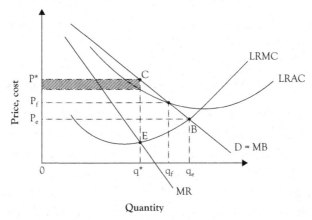

Figure 7-13. Natural monopoly and regulation.

intersection of marginal revenue and marginal cost. The firm is earning an economic profit and failing to produce electricity at the allocatively efficient output level (q_e) where marginal benefit equals marginal cost. The deadweight welfare loss created by the monopolist is the area CEB.

Society, through government action, has a range of options. It can let things be and accept the situation; it can break up the monopoly (losing all of the cost-saving advantages of economies of scale) and allow the entry of several small competitors ("baby" Sparxs); or it can regulate the existing monopoly. If it chooses regulation, society still must make choices. Ought it require the firm to generate electricity at the allocatively efficient output level or, if not at that level, where?

Socially Optimal Output Level (P = LRMC)

One option is that the monopolist is regulated in order to achieve the socially optimal output level (q_e). To do this, the firm would be required to produce level q_e units of output, where marginal benefit equals marginal cost. However, in order to drum up sufficient demand to absorb this amount of production, the firm's price would have to be reduced to P_e.

This strategy poses a problem—at P_e, the price is lower than average cost and the firm will earn a negative economic profit. The owners of this firm will not tolerate this—remember that this is a long-run situation—and will quit the industry in search of a fair return on their investment elsewhere. Society, then, will have no electricity!

Sparx's loss per unit of electricity generated is equal to the vertical gap between P_e and LRAC at q_e. Society could "fill the gap" by offering the company a subsidy that fully compensates for the loss. Economically, this might be feasible, but, politically, may be imprudent.

THINK IT THROUGH: Sparx, a long-term monopoly that has been extracting economic profits from its customers for years by withholding output and charging high prices is now seen by tax-paying voters to be receiving subsidies, financed by tax hikes. The higher taxes may be borne by those same long-suffering customers or, if not, there is an income redistribution away from taxpayers and to the monopoly's customers. Either way, despite lower prices and improved service, there is a political risk that voters will rebel. Some students may feel they see connections between this scenario and President Obama's managed health care system.

174 A PRIMER ON MICROECONOMICS

Fair Return Output Level (P = LRAC)

A compromise option that is frequently employed in regulation is to control the firm's output and price in such a way that the original deadweight welfare loss (CEB) is reduced, but not eradicated. "Fair return" (or average cost) pricing sets the firm's price so that the firm breaks even. If the price is set at P_f, where it equals average cost, then, on average, the firm will earn zero economic profit. By earning a reasonable rate of return (a normal profit) for its owners, Sparx will continue to operate without requiring a subsidy from taxpayers. Output will be higher than q* and price will be lower than P*.

Problems With Regulation

Controlling a natural monopoly presents particular problems. If a fair return is guaranteed, then there is little incentive to be diligent in cutting costs, boosting productivity, or innovating. Cost-saving initiatives translate into lower future rates. Reversing this point, regulated industries display the **Averch–Johnson effect**, which is the tendency for regulated firms to accumulate an overabundance of capital. If the firm's rate of return is based on the quantity of its capital, then there is an incentive to increase investment. Although this may be rationalized as a desire to provide a high-quality service—in the case of an electric firm, for example, fewer outages because of the additional generating capacity—the consequence is that the firm is driven away from the socially optimal level. Efficiency is sacrificed to profit.

   Regulatory capture suggests that, because of close association over time, the role of a regulatory agency may shift from being a watchdog for the interests of customers to being a lapdog for the interests of the industry, with inefficient or undesirable practices being supported or, at least, ignored.

THINK IT THROUGH: There are frequent claims of regulators being "in bed" with the executives of large firms—perhaps the most notable recent example is the series of "lapses" in scrutiny that led to the meltdown on Wall Street in 2007–2008 and the subsequent Great Recession. The Food and Drug Administration has been accused of promoting the interests of agribusiness over that of consumer health, for example, in the continued use by milk producers of the growth hormone rBGH, which has been linked to cancer and has been banned in the European Union, Canada, and Australia.

The Interstate Commerce Commission was accused by its critics of sympathetically setting railroad freight rates and trucking rates at high levels and of acting to exclude competition through restrictive practices. The ICC was scrapped in 1995—subsequently, railroad freight rates and trucking rates have fallen by about 50 percent.

Applications: Cable TV, NFL Logos, and Electricity Generation

This section considers three examples of industries or firms whose practices have attracted the scrutiny of regulators.

Cable TV

It is frequently claimed that the cable TV industry is an example of a natural monopoly. With expensive cable to be laid, there are high initial costs to set up the system but relatively low variable costs once the system is in operation. This implies that the average cost decreases as the number of subscribers increases—a hallmark of a natural monopoly. Given that cable TV in a local region is a natural monopoly, and during most of its history it has been treated as such, then why is it beneficial to prevent competition in this case?

The argument goes that having more than one cable provider competing in a market would lead to wasteful duplication of service, economies of scale would be reduced and average costs of production would increase.

Cable TV rates were deregulated in 1984 when price caps were removed. This policy change had several effects—prices for cable TV subscribers increased but, because more channels and better quality programming was made available, the number of subscribers increased. Cable was re-regulated in 1992, but only partially. Pricing on basic packages was controlled, to ensure that viewers could afford television access, but premium channels were not subject to regulation. The result was predictable—cable companies provided mediocre "basic" packages and tried to tempt subscribers to the far more attractive premium packages. Currently, only "basic tier" cable TV is regulated.

Cable TV has so far been successful in bundling channels together—to get a particular channel such as HBO the customer must also subscribe to channels that they do not wish to have. The *à la carte* alternative, in which subscribers can pick and pay for only those channels they wish to have, has been resisted as requiring very expensive technology.

Is Bundling Desirable? Bundling, the practice where the firm offers a take-it-or-leave-it choice of channels, is economically sensible from the viewpoint of the provider—given that providing additional channels involves a low marginal cost.

Suppose Cabal Cable has two subscribers, Lionel and Nancy. Lionel values ESPN at $4.00 per month and MTV at $3.00 per month whereas Nancy values ESPN at $3.00 per month and MTV at $4.00 per month. With *à la carte* pricing, Cabal's revenues would be maximized if each channel cost $3.00 per month because each individual would buy ESPN and MTV, spending $6.00 each. Cabal's total revenue would be $12.00.

THINK IT THROUGH: If Cabal raised the price per channel to more than $3.00 per month, then Lionel would not wish to subscribe to MTV and Nancy would not wish to subscribe to ESPN.

The two-channel bundle is worth $7.00 per month to Lionel and is worth $7.00 per month to Nancy. If Cabal offers the bundle at $7.00 per month, then both viewers will subscribe, increasing Cabal's revenue to $14.00. If the cost of adding a subscriber to an established channel is zero (or negligible) then offering the bundle increases Cabal's profitability.

Bundling may also benefit the subscriber. Instead of paying two charges to receive two desired but separate *à la carte* channels, one lower fee may secure both desired channels. If Cabal offers its bundle at a rate of $6.50 per month, Lionel and Nancy will each receive a consumer surplus of 50 cents per month.

NFL and Apparel Logos

In 2010, there was an antitrust case concerning the NFL's practice of having an exclusive licensing agreement and negotiating as a single unit with apparel companies that wished to market NFL team logos. The NFL's position was that significant competition existed between NFL teams and also that there was significant competition between the NFL and other forms of entertainment. The court rejected this argument, however, finding that team logos were not good substitutes for one another (would a Giants fan really wish to buy a Carolina Panthers t-shirt?) and that the NFL's exclusive licensing agreement, in which teams operated collectively, violated antitrust rules because the collective action had the consequence of driving up licensing revenues.

Electricity Generation and Deregulation

Enthusiasm for regulation swings like a pendulum. Following the financial missteps revealed by the meltdown on Wall Street in 2008 and the bursting of the housing bubble, calls for more stringent regulation have increased in volume. In earlier decades, deregulation was more favored. Deregulation in the airline industry reduced fares by about one-third, and telephone service became cheaper.

Deregulation can go seriously wrong, however, as the following case demonstrates and, when it does, it can swing the pendulum in the opposite direction. In 1998, California deregulated its wholesale electricity prices and prices began to rise. This was due to an extraordinary and unforeseeable alignment of supply and demand factors—aging generating capacity, and declines in water to power hydroelectric plants on the supply side, and an economic boom, rising population, and hot summer weather boosting demand.

Electricity generating firms were quick to realize that, if supply were curtailed, then the price of electricity would rise sharply, given an inelastic demand. Demand for electricity is inelastic because there are few substitutes and it is highly costly to store for later use.

THINK IT THROUGH: In Chapter 4, we discussed the Total Revenue Test as a method of determining whether the demand for a product was inelastic or not. We concluded that, if demand were inelastic, then an increase in price would cause total revenue to increase. Clearly, the electricity producers had some economics majors on their payroll because they realized that, by cutting supply, the price of their product would increase and their total revenue would also increase.

In order to reduce supply and drive up prices and revenue, many plants were closed down for "maintenance" during periods of peak demand, widespread blackouts occurred and wholesale electricity prices increased, sometimes by tenfold. California's governor initiated a state of emergency that lasted for more than two years.

Unfortunately, the transmission and distribution of electricity for retail customers had not been deregulated so companies such as Pacific Gas and Electric were being forced to buy electricity at high unregulated prices and sell to customers at low regulated prices. Pacific Gas and Electric filed for bankruptcy in 2001. It was only with the bankruptcy of Enron, an energy-trader and major player in the manipulation of the wholesale electricity market, that the situation began to stabilize.

Because of California's experience, several states have reversed their moves toward electricity deregulation, while California now requires electricity distributors to acquire their own generating capacity, in order to prevent reliance on independent electricity-generating firms.

Review: In general, monopoly misallocates society's scarce resources but this need not always be true—perfect price discrimination may result in an allocatively efficient result, and natural monopoly's cost-saving economies may trump perfect competition. Further, in the case of a regulated monopoly, the cure may be almost as injurious to efficiency as the cause.

CHAPTER 8

Between Perfect Competition and Monopoly

By the end of this chapter you will be able to:

1. Identify the features of a monopolistically competitive firm and industry.
2. Define product differentiation and explain how it occurs.
3. Explain why the monopolistically competitive firm will make only normal profits in long-run equilibrium.
4. Identify and analyze the factors in monopolistic competition that cause inefficiency and resource misallocation.
5. Identify the characteristics of an oligopolistic firm and industry.
6. Discuss the behavioral implications of the cartel model and the price leadership model.
7. Outline the kinked demand curve model and explain how it explains price stickiness.
8. Describe ways in which an oligopolistic industry may be inefficient.
9. Describe how the contestable market model affects the perspective on oligopolistic inefficiency.
10. Use game theory to analyze the strategies available to rivals in a two-person game.
11. Explain what the Herfindahl–Hirschman Index is and how it is used in antitrust cases.

When you visit the Food Court at your local mall, dozens of businesses vie with one another to attract you (and your wallet). Similarly, clothing stores, shoe stores, and electronics stores await beyond the Food Court. None of these firms is perfectly competitive; none is a monopoly. The presence of advertising and brand names places these firms outside the perfectly competitive model and the presence of close substitutes places them beyond the bounds of pure monopoly. These firms are either monopolistically competitive or oligopolistic in nature. What distinguishes firms such as these, and how well do they cater to our needs?

Chapter Preview: In Chapters 5 and 6, we set up and examined "perfect competition," a model of a market that assumes many firms with free entry into the market. We discovered that, in general, perfectly competitive markets serve society's needs very effectively. In Chapter 7, we moved to the other extreme, looking at "monopoly" industry, wherein there is only one firm, which preserves its unique position through the imposition of substantial barriers to entry. With some qualifications, we concluded that monopoly does not usually serve society well.

Most firms, however, operate in neither a perfectly competitive environment nor a monopolistic one. In this chapter, we look at the two intermediate "market structures" of monopolistic competition and oligopoly and assess how effectively they address the issues of productive efficiency and allocative efficiency.

Economists who study industrial organization use three broad categories for their investigations into an industry's behavior—market structure, conduct, and performance. *Market structure* considers issues such as the number of firms, the significance of substantial economies of scale, and how dominant the four, or eight, largest firms are. *Conduct* examines how firms behave, how prices are set, and whether firms advertise. *Performance* turns on the consideration of efficiency. Keep these issues in mind as we explore monopolistic competition and oligopoly.

Brain Teaser: If you were to open a restaurant in your town, which factors would be of most concern to you to help you make your venture a success? Specifically, how would you go about cultivating a clientele and establish your identity in the market? What choices would you have to make? What methods and media might you use to differentiate your product? How closely would you monitor the activities of your competitors? By the end of this chapter, determine whether your restaurant is part of an oligopoly or is monopolistically competitive in nature.

Monopolistic Competition: Perfect Competition with Differentiated Products

Characteristics of Monopolistic Competition

Like perfect competition, a monopolistically competitive industry contains a large number of small firms operating independently of one another. Unlike perfect competition, each firm faces a highly elastic (but not perfectly elastic) demand because each firm is selling a product for which there are a number of close substitutes—restaurants are an excellent example of monopolistic competition. Consumers are sensitive to prices, but, because there is some degree of product differentiation, each firm does have some limited ability to adjust its price. There are few barriers to entry in monopolistic competition, so, in the long run, it is fairly easy to enter a monopolistically competitive industry. Firms in monopolistically competitive industries do not benefit from substantial economies of scale.

Production Differentiation

The perfectly competitive firm has nothing to advertise—each firm sells the identical product at exactly the same price. In contrast, the monopolistically competitive firm is keen to make potential customers aware of the special features of its own product or service—product differentiation is a hallmark of monopolistic competition. Product differentiation occurs when a product is distinguished from its alternatives in some positive way in the minds of consumers.

THINK IT THROUGH: What might help distinguish one company's product from that of its rivals? Advertising in all its forms—billboards, junk mail, radio and TV jingles—can let consumers know what options are available and may also shape their preferences. Radio stations become known for a particular style of music—country, rock, gospel. Restaurants offer specialized cuisines—Chinese, French, seafood—and may signal this by the choice of the restaurant's name. Brand names, to be sure, reinforced through advertising, may be an important factor in determining a customer's choice. Location, hours of operation, expertise, credit facilities, and so on, may all be features that distinguish one firm from its rivals. Higher quality of product may be signaled through higher prices or by celebrity endorsements or testimonials from "satisfied" customers. Can you think of other distinguishing features?

Monopolistic Competition in the Short Run: The Four Short-Run Cases Revisited

When we looked at perfect competition in Chapter 5, we found that the firm's "short-run cost picture" was determined by the "specialization effect" and the "congestion effect." There is nothing new to learn on the cost side of the analysis. The monopolistically competitive firm experiences similar effects and has a similar short-run cost picture, as shown in Figure 8-1.

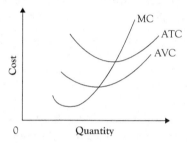

Figure 8-1. The monopolistic competitor's short-run cost picture.

Similarly, there is nothing new to learn on the revenue side of the analysis. Because it has some control over the price it may charge for its (somewhat differentiated) product, the firm's "revenue picture" is, in principle, the same as that for a monopolist—a downward-sloping demand curve, with an associated marginal revenue (MR) curve, as shown in Figure 8-2.

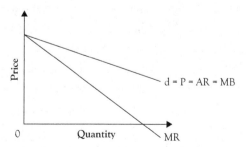

Figure 8-2. The monopolistic competitor's revenue picture.

Clearly, we are recycling established concepts! All the definitions and relationships we set out in previous chapters still hold true. The firm's demand curve, to be sure, is much more elastic than that faced by the monopolist but, because the demand curve is negatively sloped, the behavior of marginal revenue is specified.

As in perfect competition and in monopoly, there are four short-run cases for the firm in this market structure. The firm can earn an economic profit, break even, incur an economic loss but produce, or shut down. Just like the perfectly competitive firm and the monopolist, the monopolistic competitor will follow the profit-maximizing procedure presented in Chapter 5. The diagrams we used to consider the four "short-run cases" for the monopolist in Chapter 7 can be reused for the monopolistically competitive firm. The elasticity of the demand curve is different but the appearance of the diagrams is the same.

THINK IT THROUGH: You should be able to draw the four "short-run cases" yourself by this time. However, if you cannot, Figure 7-5 through Figure 7-8 are the ones you require.

Monopolistic Competition in the Long Run

When we consider the long run, it is the similarity between monopolistic competition and perfect competition that is more pertinent. In both market structures, it is fairly easy for firms to enter or leave the industry in the long run. Because of this, the typical monopolistically competitive firm will earn only a normal profit in long-run equilibrium.

Consider a small town with, say, ten restaurants offering a mixture of different cuisines. Initially, each firm is earning a normal profit. However, consumer demand increases for some reason—for example, there is increased affluence, an influx of new residents, a change in preferences away from home-prepared meals. The demand curve faced by the typical firm ("Adam's Ribs and Bar-B-Q") shifts to the right, and each of the ten restaurants now earns a (short-run) profit. The new demand curve is shown as d_1 in Figure 8-3. The associated marginal revenue curve is MR_1.

Producing at the output level (q_1) where MR = MC, the firm will set a price of P_1 and earn an economic profit as shown by the shaded area in the diagram. Attracted by the higher-than-normal profits, new firms enter

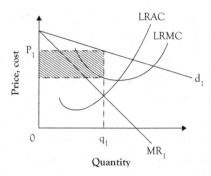

Figure 8-3. The long-run equilibrium process.

the industry in the long run. The opening of new restaurants in town has two effects on Adam's Ribs. First, his market share will be diminished. If there are now 20 restaurants instead of 10, then Adam's market share will have decreased from ten percent to five percent. This shows up as a leftward shift of Adam's demand curve. Second, because patrons now have more—and closer—choices than before, the price elasticity of demand for Adam's Ribs will increase. Whereas previously there may have been no other barbecue restaurants in town, it is now more likely that a close rival will be present. Customers can be choosier.

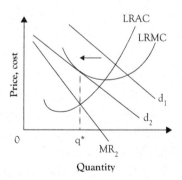

Figure 8-4. Long-run equilibrium.

Firms will continue to enter the industry as long as economic profits exist and Adam's demand curve will be forced farther to the left. The process will stop only when the typical firm's demand curve (d_2) is tangent to the long-run average cost curve as shown in Figure 8-4. If the industry "overshoots" by having too many firms enter the industry, then each firm's demand curve will be pushed too far to the left, losses will be incurred, causing some firms to leave the industry and the demand curve of each surviving firm to shift back to the right until a normal profit is earned at an output level, q*, and a price, P*. As with perfect competition, it is the condition of easy entry and exit that guarantees that only a normal profit will be earned in long-run equilibrium.

The Monopolistic Competitor and Performance Criteria

In long-run equilibrium, the firm's output level is q* and its price is P* as shown in Figure 8-4. Turning our attention to the three performance criteria we developed in Chapter 6, we can see that, although the typical firm does earn only a normal profit (Criterion 1), it is neither productively efficient (Criterion 2) nor allocatively efficient (Criterion 3) and, therefore, appears inferior to perfect competition. Consider Figure 8-5.

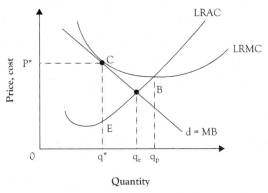

Figure 8-5. Long-run equilibrium and efficiency.

Productive efficiency: A firm is deemed to be productively efficient if it produces at the minimum point on the long-run average cost curve. In Figure 8-5, this occurs at the output level, q_p. The monopolistically competitive firm in long-run equilibrium, which will choose to restrict output to q*, therefore, is not productively efficient. Relative to perfect competition, monopolistic competition fails to pass muster. Because the firm (and industry) is failing to take full advantage of economies of scale, it can be argued that the monopolistically competitive industry suffers from excess capacity. Given the overall level of demand, if there were fewer firms, each with a somewhat higher level of output, then the product's unit costs would be reduced and scarce resources could be reallocated. Monopolistic competition, it could be argued, underutilizes and squanders our scarce resources.

Monopolistically competitive industries suffer from excess capacity and, in the previous paragraph, we argued that this is inefficient. But it is? Consider what is implied for the customer by the presence of excess capacity. When your car breaks down, you wish for instant service from the mechanic, not a two-week delay. At the restaurant, the customer wishes to be seated immediately instead of having to queue with a beeper. Once seated, the customer's preference is not to be surrounded by other tables and chairs, hordes of other diners (and their children), overworked wait-staff, and the sense that one should eat up and get out as quickly as possible because the table is needed for the next customer. We prefer service and choice and, if it is inefficient to have mechanics, plumbers, and restaurants waiting with idle resources for us to decide to call on their services, then so be it! Similarly, it would be most frugal with resources if we all wore the same style and color of "one size fits all" clothing, but we are willing to sacrifice efficiency for choice and individuality. And, beyond all other market structures, choice is what monopolistic competition delivers.

Allocative efficiency: A firm is allocatively efficient if it produces at the output level where price (marginal benefit) equals long-run marginal cost. In Figure 8-5, this output level is q_e. Again, the firm, in pursuit of profit, will opt to produce at the lower output level, q^*. The deadweight loss of this choice is the area CEB.

The general theme of our theoretical argument is that, like monopoly, monopolistic competition is inefficient relative to perfect competition. However, against that conclusion, we must set the fact that monopolistic competition offers abundant variety that appeals to our individualism. Also, we must not forget the issue of product innovation. Much of the innovation in American industry springs from basement inventors and weekend hobbyists whose interests and skills carry them to develop new products or new twists on existing products. Giants such as Bill Gates and Steve Jobs once were "small" innovators and Facebook began as a dormroom experiment. There is little incentive to innovate in perfect competition because no form of product differentiation, such as branding or trademarks, is possible. Similarly, the monopolist has little wish to shake up his market with new products. Although large oligopolistic firms indulge in research and development programs, many of the patents granted by the Patent Office are the result of the activities of small entrepreneurs with big dreams.

Review of Monopolistic Competition

Monopoly has *one* firm, oligopoly (as we shall see) has a *few*, perfect competition and monopolistic competition *many*. Monopolistic competition's distinguishing characteristic is product differentiation—the monopolistically competitive firm lives and dies by its ability to attract customers in a crowded marketplace. Despite the downward-sloping demand and marginal revenue curves, the short-run and long-run equilibration stories for perfectly competitive and monopolistically competitive firms are very similar. Monopolistic competition differs from monopoly and oligopoly in that firms in monopolistically competitive industries can't influence the market price by virtue of their size. Relative to perfect competition, the presence of monopolistic competition bestows variety for the consumer but with higher-than-necessary costs and a deadweight loss.

Brain Teaser Solution: Almost certainly your restaurant will be monopolistically competitive—with many close substitutes, low barriers to entry, and highly elastic demand. Product differentiation ought to be important to you and knowledge of local market conditions may be critical to your survival. Note that your restaurant is selling not only food— you are offering an entire "dining experience" that will include elements such as location, decor, and quality of service.

Oligopoly: Burgers, Banking, and Beer

The final of the four market structures—oligopoly—lies closer to monopoly than to perfect competition and, sometimes, oligopolistic firms find it advantageous to group together into a *cartel* and behave, in effect, like a monopoly in order to maximize their joint profits. In other cases, competition between rivals may be aggressive—burger wars, for instance. In other industries, firms may deemphasize rivalry, preferring less-threatening methods of attracting customers.

THINK IT THROUGH: If you wish to identify probable oligopolists, think about the sponsors of "big" events, such as the Superbowl or the Olympics, or the advertisers in *Time* or *Newsweek*. Almost certainly, the firms you see are in oligopolistic industries.

Characteristics of Oligopoly

An oligopolistic industry has a "few" large interdependent firms within a market—the market may be local, national, or international. Usually (but not always), each firm has substantial market power and can impose strong barriers to entry, often because of significant economies of scale. Products may be differentiated (cars or burgers) or standardized (oil and other chemicals). Firms may compete in terms of price or they may not. A key characteristic of oligopoly is *mutual interdependence*—the behavior of each firm affects and depends on the expected reactions of its rivals. Because each firm's actions depend on the expected reactions of its rivals, this market structure requires complex analysis and several models have been developed.

Short-Run Cases and Long-Run Equilibrium

The models that follow may look quite different from those in the previous chapters, but the relevant principles remain unchanged. As with the other market structures, the oligopolistic firm faces four possible "short-run cases," and will apply the same techniques as we saw firms in the other markets use in order to deal with each eventuality. Because of substantial barriers to entry, we would expect to see firms earning an economic profit in long-run equilibrium—just like monopoly—although, in the case of contestable markets discussed as follows, this may not occur.

When an oligopoly consists of only two firms it is called a *duopoly*. Suppose that you sell ice cream in a two-dimensional world, such as a stretch of beach, as shown in Figure 8-6. The "market" is 200 yards long and potential customers are evenly distributed along the beach. You plan

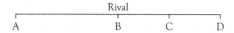

Figure 8-6. Duopoly at the beach.

to set up your stall at the midpoint of the beach in order to maximize sales. However, when you arrive, you discover that a rival has already claimed that prime location! Where should you set up now? Should you move farther along the beach?

Consider Figure 8-6. If you should set up beside your competitor at Point B, then each seller will receive 50 percent of the market, assuming that prices and the products are comparable. Moving away from the midpoint to, for example, Point D, gives your rival 75 percent of the market whereas you will attract only the 25 percent between Point D and Point C. Consumers between Point A and Point B will buy from your rival, as will those between Point B and Point C. Wherever your rival locates, you should locate right beside him but closer to Point B. If he locates at Point D, then you should set up just marginally closer to the midpoint of the beach. The sellers are mutually interdependent.

Explicit Collusion—Cartels

The simplest form of oligopoly to analyze is the cartel. A cartel is a group of producers that have come together to determine price and output in order to maximize joint profits—OPEC (the Organization of Petroleum Exporting Countries) is the most widely known example. The drive to form a cartel may come from firms wishing to collude in order to prevent the risk of potentially destructive competition. However, when a cartel is operating, although it may be beneficial to the members, all the adverse effects of monopoly will ensue—consumers will pay monopoly prices, firms will reap monopoly profits, consumer surplus will be reduced, and deadweight losses will occur. Worse still, because the cartel's members produce separately, they do *not* create the cost-saving benefits that derive from economies of scale that an actual monopoly would generate. Cartels represent the worst of all possible worlds for the consumer, and price-fixing collusion is illegal under United States' antitrust laws.

In New York, milk and Italian bread have been examples of collusion—a few powerful firms conspiring to keep prices high. The milk cartel survived for 50 years and, following its demise, the price of a gallon of milk tumbled by 30 percent.

OPEC has been a successful and long-lived international cartel, but longevity such as OPEC and the milk cartel exhibit is rare. The larger the number of firms and the more diverse their production costs and objectives (some oil-producing countries, for example, wish for rapid exploitation of their resources while others prefer a longer-term approach), the more difficult it is to reach an agreement and to perpetuate it. Policing is important. If the agreement is to work properly, each member must produce no more than the amount of product stipulated. There may be a strong temptation to cheat, either by offering covert discounted prices, or by increasing production and selling secretly, or both. Once cartel members begin even to suspect cheating, the agreement is likely to unravel.

Tacit Collusion—Price Leadership

Explicit collusion is illegal in the United States but *tacit collusion* operates in a gray area. Tacit collusion occurs when firms arrive at an "understanding," perhaps without direct discussion, and can be an attractive strategy to avoid price competition and to maintain profits. Such "gentlemen's agreements" are illegal but are often difficult to prove. It's not surprising that real-world examples of collusion continue to surface. Some years ago, several Ivy League universities were accused of price-fixing by sharing information about qualified students and agreeing not to compete on offers of financial aid to them. The universities, which consented to terminate the practices, justified their practices by claiming that, by preventing competition, they were allowing the students to choose the institution that best matched their academic needs.

Price leadership involves implicit coordination between firms, with a dominant firm, often the largest or most efficient firm, setting its price and the remaining firms following its lead. For many years, Bank of America would announce interest rate changes and its rivals would follow the pattern it had established. Similarly, U. S. Steel, for many years the dominant firm in the steel industry, set the pace for its competitors with orderly price adjustments. Usually, such price changes are infrequent, clearly announced, and nonaggressive.

Price leadership has survival value. Each oligopolist controls a sizeable portion of the market and can be a formidable opponent, so a full-blown price war is a perilous activity that can be expensive for all and may be destructive for some—far better to signal intentions in a clear and structured manner.

Kinked Demand Curve Model

Given the risk involved for an oligopolist in changing her price independently of her rivals, prices in oligopolistic markets might be expected to be "sticky," that is, not subject to frequent adjustments. The kinked demand curve model has been developed to analyze this phenomenon.

Consider Figure 8-7. Point A shows the current price ($20) and output (1,000) for an oligopolist—Olga. Point A must be on Olga's demand curve. What if Olga lowers her price to $19? We would expect quantity demanded of Olga's product to increase but the number of new customers attracted to Olga will depend on the reaction of her rivals. If the rivals do not respond to Olga's price cut, then her product will have become relatively attractive (elastic) and there will be a substantial increase in quantity demanded, perhaps from 1,000 to 1,500. Demand curve d_{NR} is Olga's demand curve when there is "no reaction" from rivals to a price change. MR_{NR} is the associated marginal revenue curve.

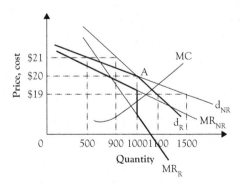

Figure 8-7. The kinked demand curve model.

If, however, rivals react to Olga's price decrease by cutting their prices by an equivalent amount, then Olga will experience a less vigorous increase in quantity demanded, perhaps from 1,000 to 1,100. Demand curve d_R is Olga's demand curve when there is a "reaction" from rivals to a price change and MR_R is the associated marginal revenue curve.

If Olga is at Point A and then raises her price from $20 to $21 but her rivals respond by raising their prices by a comparable amount, then Olga will lose a few customers who have been priced out of the market— demand will be relatively inelastic and quantity demanded might shrink from 1,000 to 900. Again, demand curve d_R is Olga's (relatively inelastic) demand curve when her rivals react to a price change. If Olga raises her price from $20 to $21 and her rivals do not respond, then Olga is likely to see quantity demanded shrink substantially (from 1,000 to 500) as many of her customers move over to her cheaper rivals. As before, demand curve d_{NR} is Olga's (relatively elastic) demand curve when her rivals do not react to a price change.

Paul Sweezy, the originator of the kinked demand curve model, then postulated that, when considering a price change, the oligopolist would assume the worst possible outcome. If Olga cuts her price, the worst outcome for her is that her rivals will reciprocate—demand curve d_{NR} is the demand curve she will face at prices less than $20. If she raises her price, the worst outcome is that her rivals do not reciprocate—demand curve d_R is the relevant demand curve at prices above than $20. The presumed demand curve, then, has a kink in it at the current price and the associated marginal revenue curve has a vertical "gap" at the current quantity, q^*.

THINK IT THROUGH (MATH): The "gap" is caused by the marginal revenue curves missing each other. However, because they have differing slopes, is it possible for the two MR curves to behave in such a manner that the discontinuity might disappear? The simple answer to this question is "no." If the demand curves have slopes as shown, then the discontinuity in the MR curve must occur—although a formal proof would take us far beyond the scope of this little book. Recall that the marginal revenue curve begins at the same point on the vertical axis as its associated demand curve and it is twice as steep as the demand curve. More complex math aside, this guarantees the presence of the gap.

The discontinuity within the MR curve is the key to explaining price stickiness. From Chapter 5, we know that the profit-maximizing firm will produce at the output level where marginal revenue equals marginal cost. It must be the case, therefore, that Olga's marginal cost curve passes through that gap—if not, then "MR = MC" would occur at a different level of output. Refer to Figure 8-7. We also know that an increase in (variable) costs will cause the marginal cost curve to shift upwards. For any other market structure, if the marginal cost curve shifts upwards, it will cause the profit-maximizing output level to decrease because the "MR = MC" intersection has changed position. In the present model, however, the marginal cost curve can shift upwards and, as long as it remains within the discontinuity, neither the profit-maximizing output level nor the profit-maximizing price will change. In the face of changing costs, price will be "sticky."

Contestable Markets

In the oligopoly models we have considered thus far, the inefficiency charges that we leveled at "artificial" monopoly can be restated with equal or greater plausibility. A brief examination of Figures 8-5 and 8-6 shows that we should expect oligopolistic firms to be allocatively inefficient and productively inefficient. In addition, many oligopolistic industries— cigarettes, beer, cars, burgers—use resources to advertise heavily, partly as a further barrier to entry.

There is one bright spot for proponents of oligopoly—the case of contestable markets. Contestable markets can arise in any market structure when the threat of entry by potential rivals is high, including oligopoly. As with perfect competition, entry into or exit from a particular market is virtually costless, perhaps because the industry's capital stock is very mobile—the airline industry is the standard example. If new profit opportunities emerge in one market—for example, the route from San Francisco to Vancouver during the 2010 Winter Olympics or the demographic shift favoring the Sun Belt, for instance—then capital will flow in that direction until the profits are competed away. Because of the threat of easy entry into and exit from a particular market, oligopolists in perfectly contestable markets perform like perfectly competitive firms—reducing prices, earning only normal profits in the long run, and cutting costs to the bone.

THINK IT THROUGH: There is a subtle point at play in our consideration of contestable markets—it is the *threat* of competition that is sufficient to make firms behave competitively, even if only one firm is actually supplying the market.

THINK IT THROUGH: Customer loyalty plans such as frequent flyer discounts, which bestow benefits on customers who do not switch between providers, have the effect of reducing contestability and preserving profits. The corollary of this tactic—imposing costs on customers who do switch providers—also functions to disincentivize shopping around. The presence of either plan suggests that a market is contestable.

Game Theory

You may have seen the Russell Crowe movie, "A Beautiful Mind," about mathematician and economist John Nash who was responsible for introducing game theory into economics. Game theory analyzes how players might react to the actions of opponents, given certain rules of conduct and potential payoffs (rewards). Because the behavior of one firm affects the fortunes of its rivals, this approach applies easily to oligopoly.

The Prisoners' Dilemma

One familiar scenario is known as the "prisoners' dilemma." In this game, each prisoner must decide whether it is in his or her own best interests to confess to a crime or to stonewall. Consider Figure 8-8, which shows the payoff matrix (in this case, a punishment matrix) facing the two perpetrators—Bonnie and Clyde.

The police tell Bonnie that, if she confesses to the bank heist but Clyde does not confess, then the charge will be reduced to two years for her, but he will get a ten-stretch. If both confess, then each will get six years. If neither confesses, then they both get five years, because there may be other evidence to link them to the crime.

If both prisoners wish to minimize the damage that the other can do to them, they both should confess. From Bonnie's viewpoint, Clyde may confess or may not confess. If Clyde confesses then, to minimize her sentence, Bonnie should also confess—six years is better than ten years. If, however, Clyde doesn't confess, then it is still in Bonnie's best interest

		Clyde's Action	
		Don't Confess	Confess
Bonnie's Action	Don't Confess	Both 4 years	Clyde gets 2 years Bonnie gets 10 years
	Confess	Clyde gets 10 years Bonnie gets 2 years	Both get 6 years in jail

Figure 8-8. The prisoners' dilemma.

to confess. If she confesses then she'll get two years but, if she doesn't, then she'll get four years.

Confessing, then, is Bonnie's best option regardless of Clyde's decision. An action is known as a **dominant strategy** if it is the best option regardless of the decision of the other party. In this example, the dominant strategy for both Bonnie and Clyde is to confess. Given the actions of the rival, if each player employs the best strategy, then the result is known as a **Nash (or non-cooperative) equilibrium**. The important point to note is that, by each individual pursuing his or her own self-interest (trying to minimize their own jail time), both individuals receive longer sentences.

Honor Among Thieves?

Clearly, it would be better for both Bonnie and Clyde if they could agree to stonewall, because then both would get four years. If the prisoners trusted each other to look after their common interests or if an underworld code of conduct—"don't rat on your friends"—were vigorously adhered to, then stonewalling would seem to be preferred. However, it would then be in Bonnie's best interest to pretend to stonewall (in order to ensure that Clyde did not confess), and then confess anyway. The more strongly that Bonnie suspects that Clyde will cheat by confessing, the greater the likelihood that she, herself, will cheat.

Application of Game Theory to Oligopoly

Let us suppose we have a soft-drinks duopoly, with PensaCola and Okra-Coke as the two firms. Each firm must decide whether or not to maintain or end an expensive advertising campaign. If both companies continue to

		PensaCola's Action	
		Don't Advertise	Advertise
OkraCoke's Action	Don't Advertise	OkraCoke: +$500 million PensaCola: +$500 million	OkraCoke: +$100 million PensaCola: +$700 million
	Advertise	OkraCoke: +$700 million PensaCola: +$100 million	OkraCoke: +$200 million PensaCola: +$200 million

Figure 8-9. Soda wars.

advertise, then the two campaigns will attract customers, and profits will be $200 million for each company. If both firms abandon their advertising campaigns then, because of the cost saving, profits will be $500 million for each company. If PensaCola advertises and OkraCoke does not, then Pensacola's profit will be $700 million whereas OkraCoke's will be $100 million. The payoffs are shown in Figure 8-9.

This is similar to the previous example in that each company has a dominant strategy and that strategy is to continue to advertise. If PensaCola stops its campaign, then OkraCoke should still advertise—$700 million is better than $500 million. If, however, PensaCola does continue to advertise, then OkraCoke should also persist—$200 million is preferable to $200 million. The Nash equilibrium is in the lower right-hand cell of the matrix.

Collusion

Self-interested behavior has led PensaCola and OkraCoke to pursue a strategy (advertising) that has reduced their joint profits. If the two firms could collude and agree not to advertise, then their joint profits would increase from $400 million to $1,000 million. Because of the suspicion that the other firm might cheat and advertise anyway, this option is unlikely to go forward unless the agreement can be assured. In fact, in the 1970s, the cigarette industry achieved just this result by strongly supporting moves that led Congress to ban cigarette ads from television.

THINK IT THROUGH: Must there always be a dominant strategy for a player?

It is possible that a player may not have a dominant strategy—one that is best regardless of the action of his rival. Suppose that, if PensaCola did not advertise, then OkraCoke's profits when advertising were $400 million (instead of $500 million). The payoffs are shown in Figure 8-10.

		PensaCola's Action	
		Don't Advertise	Advertise
OkraCoke's Action	Don't Advertise	OkraCoke: +$500 million PensaCola: +$500 million	OkraCoke: +$100 million PensaCola: +$700 million
	Advertise	OkraCoke: +$400 million PensaCola: +$100 million	OkraCoke: +$200 million PensaCola: +$200 million

Figure 8-10. Soda wars revisited.

In this case, OkraCoke would gain more by refraining from advertising, so what should the executives at OkraCoke do? Advertise! OkraCoke can expect its rival to follow its dominant strategy and PensaCola's dominant strategy is to advertise. Because PensaCola can be counted on to advertise, OkraCoke will advertise, because $200 million is preferable to $100 million.

Price Stickiness and Game Theory

When we examined the kinked demand curve model, we met Olga, who was considering changing the price of her product. To simplify the analysis, let us suppose that Olga has only one rival (Oleg) and that they are restricted to either maintaining their current price of $20 or cutting it to $19. Currently, Olga and Oleg each have 1,000 customers and each generates $20,000 in revenue.

On the basis of Figure 8-7, we can build up a payoff matrix as shown in Figure 8-11. If Olga were to cut her price to $19 but Oleg did not, then Olga's quantity demanded would expand to 1,500 customers and her revenue would increase to $28,500. Assuming that Olga attracted the additional customers from Oleg, then his revenue would fall from $20,000 to $10,000.

		Oleg's Action	
		Cut Price	Maintain Price
Olga's Action	Cut Price	Olga's revenue $20,900	Olga's revenue $28,500
		Oleg's revenue $20,900	Oleg's revenue $10,000
	Maintain Price	Olga's revenue $10,000	Olga's revenue $20,000
		Oleg's revenue $28,500	Oleg's revenue $20,000

Figure 8-11. Revenue maximization.

If Olga were to cut her price to $19 and Oleg followed suit, then each firm would attract 100 more customers, and each would see revenue increase from $20,000 by $900 (1,100 × $19).

What should the duopolists do? For both, the dominant strategy is to cut price. By doing so, total revenue will increase from $20,000 to $20,900.

THINK IT THROUGH: From our study of elasticity in Chapter 4, we should expect total revenue to increase. We know that demand must be price-elastic, otherwise marginal revenue would not be positive. Therefore, with an elastic demand, and a decrease in price, total revenue will increase.

The kinked demand curve model suggests that the firm will wish to maintain price, not reduce it. Clearly, despite the increase in total revenue, if marginal cost increases as output expands, then total economic profit may decrease and it would be in the firms' common interest to maintain price at $20.

Repeated Games

Managers learn. If one firm makes a change in price or service and its rivals fall in line, then an expectation is built up. For example, the airline industry has progressively reduced in-flight service. Fees for checked baggage are commonplace. In banking, market leader Bank of America began charging fees for withdrawals at ATMs—other banks followed suit. Similarly, following the financial disruption of the Great Recession, Bank of America was the first to charge fees on zero-balance credit cards.

Over time, industry expectations may be established and cooperation may become easier to achieve and sustain. As the "game" is played repeatedly, participants may learn to signal intent and to accommodate each other. Rules of conduct may emerge—game theorists refer to a *tit-for-tat* strategy as a frequently developed understanding—a case of "one good (or bad) turn deserves another." Accordingly, the ability of oligopolists to maximize joint profits may be durable.

Policy Response to Oligopoly

The Clayton Act of 1914 allows the government to limit mergers that might substantially lessen competition in an industry. The Herfindahl–Hirschman Index (HHI) is a measure of market concentration and is used by the Antitrust Division of the Department of Justice as a guide to determine whether a proposed merger may be undesirable.

The HHI for an industry is calculated by taking each firm's market share, expressed as a percentage, squaring each of these values, and summing them. In an industry with four equal-sized firms, the HHI would be 2,500 ($25^2 + 25^2 + 25^2 + 25^2$). A pure monopoly would register a value of 10,000 (that is, 100^2) whereas the HHI for an industry with 100 firms, each with a market share of one percent, would be 100.

An industry with an HHI in excess of 1,800 is considered "highly concentrated." A proposed merger that would raise the HHI above 1,800 might be challenged if it would raise the industry's index by more than 50, and almost certainly would be challenged if it would raise the industry's index by more than 100. An important element of the Antitrust Division's scrutiny is whether the proposed merger will enhance the ability of firms to engage in "coordinated interaction," whether lawful or not.

Mergers in highly concentrated industries may be approved in particular circumstances such as if there is significant foreign competition, or if one of the firms is in financial trouble, or if it would enhance efficiency. Firms basing their application to merge on the claim that efficiency will be improved bear the burden of substantiating their claim.

Review of Oligopoly: Of the four market structures, oligopoly is the most difficult to pin down. Firms may or may not sell differentiated products. They may or may not advertise heavily. They may or may not earn substantial long-run economic profits. They may or may not collude, openly or otherwise. They may or may not be efficient—although they are likely not to be, except in the case of contestable markets.

An oligopolistic industry is typified by a small number of mutually interdependent firms. Game theory gives us some fresh insights into how these firms may negotiate with each other.

CHAPTER 9

Market Failures and Solutions

By the end of this chapter you will be able to:

1. Give two major sources of market failure.
2. Define what an externality is and explain why externalities are a source of market failure. Explain the terms marginal external cost, marginal social cost, and marginal private cost. Explain why social costs and private costs may differ, and give examples.
3. Draw a graph depicting a negative (positive) externality. Explain why the presence of a negative (positive) externality will lead to an over-production (underproduction) of the good.
4. List and evaluate five different methods of internalizing an externality.
5. Identify the two characteristics that distinguish public goods from private goods.
6. Explain why the free market underproduces public goods and describe a solution that will result in the efficient provision of public goods.
7. Identify the cause of the "tragedy of the commons."

Opener: In Chapter 2, we opened with a quote from George Bernard Shaw and so in this, our final chapter, it seems appropriate to refer once more to the great man's words. Shaw once remarked that, "If all the economists were laid end to end, they'd never reach a conclusion." Hopefully, by the end of this chapter, we will have proved him wrong!

Chapter Preview: In Chapter 6, we discovered perfectly competitive markets do a good job of allocating our limited resources toward the production of the goods and services we most desire. In some circumstances, however, even perfectly competitive markets fail in their task. Issues including asymmetrical information, moral hazard, and adverse selection were discussed as causes of inefficient resource allocation for freely operating markets. We briefly looked at externalities and public goods. In Chapter 7, we found that natural monopoly may be a preferable model for arranging production than perfect competition.

In this chapter, we resume our examination of the circumstances in which externalities and public goods may arise and then consider how the "market failure" can be corrected.

Externalities: Spillover Costs and Benefits

In Chapters 2 and 3, when we used demand and supply analysis to look at the operation of markets, we made an important assumption. That assumption was that all of the costs and all of the benefits involved in the production and consumption of the good or service were embodied in the demand and supply curve.

To recap: As shown in Figure 9-1, a demand curve depicts the marginal benefit received by the consumer from each successive unit consumed whereas a supply curve represents the marginal cost of producing

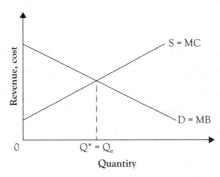

Figure 9-1. Demand, supply, profit maximization, and allocative efficiency.

each successive unit supplied. We argued that perfectly competitive firms, in their quest to find the output level that will maximize profits (Q^*), will coincidentally find themselves at the socially optimal output level of production of a good (Q_e) where the marginal benefit and marginal cost of the last unit produced are equal. We concluded, in Chapter 3, that producing up to the point where marginal benefit and marginal cost are equal maximizes the sum of consumer and producer surplus—maximizing society's total surplus.

Let us be clear on this point. The demand (marginal benefit) curve is assumed to represent all of the benefits received by society during the production and consumption of the good and the supply (marginal cost) curve is assumed to represent all of the opportunity costs imposed on society during the production and consumption of the good. But what if that assumption is false? What if there are additional benefits received by members of society or additional costs imposed on members of society by the consumption or production of a good and that these benefits or costs are not incorporated into the process that determines the profit-maximizing output level? In that case, the allocatively efficient output level will be harder to find and need not be identical to the profit-maximizing output level. In the quest for profits, it is probable that society's preferred output level, Q_e, will go by the board.

Negative Externalities

The production of a good imposes costs—opportunity costs—on the firm producing the good and these costs are reflected in the price charged when the good is sold. Similarly, the benefits received by the consumer are reflected in the price he is willing to pay. Market price, then, indicates the costs to the producer and the benefits to the consumer of the production and consumption of a good. However, in the case of a negative externality (or spillover cost), there are additional costs borne by society during the production or consumption of the good.

An externality may occur at either stage—production or consumption—and, therefore, it is useful to subdivide negative externalities into **negative externalities in production** and **negative externalities in consumption**.

Negative Externalities in Production

During the production process, the firm incurs various costs, and these costs, internalized by the firm, are reflected in its supply curve—let us call these the *marginal private costs* (MPC) of the good. Such costs are recognized, then, in the marketplace, and affect the profit-maximizing output level. Other costs may not be held internal to the firm—the costs imposed on society by pollution, for instance. Atmospheric pollution caused by a factory may impose costs on sensitive members of society, and these costs are external to the marketplace transaction—acid rain, for example, may fall on a different country or even a different continent. Let us call these the *marginal external costs* (MEC) of the good. For society, but not for the producer, the overall cost of the good—its *marginal social cost* (MSC)—is the sum of the private costs and the external costs. Our initial assumption, that there are no marginal external costs, meant that the marginal private cost curve and the marginal social cost curve were one and the same but, if this assumption is false, then the difference emerges between the MPC curve and the MSC curve.

THINK IT THROUGH: The entire issue of global warming is one of externalities. Involved parties, whose production of greenhouse gases may play a part in the planet's rising temperatures, often couch their response in terms of being willing to cooperate, except for the likelihood of losing a competitive edge. If the responsibility for treating those pollutants were to be internalized to the firm, it is contended, then its costs would rise, causing it to lose customers (perhaps to less scrupulous foreign competitors).

This point is shown graphically in Figure 9-2. At each output level, the vertical distance between the MPC curve and the MSC curve is the extent of the marginal external costs borne by society during the production or, as we shall see, the consumption of the good.

The threat that externalities pose to allocative efficiency can be seen in Figure 9-3. Left to its own devices, the market, in the shape of the demand (marginal benefit) curve and the supply (marginal private cost) curve, will set output at Q^* but the socially optimal output level—the one that takes full account of all costs and benefits—is established at the intersection of the marginal social cost curve and the marginal benefit curve, at Q_e. The perfectly competitive market is overallocating resources

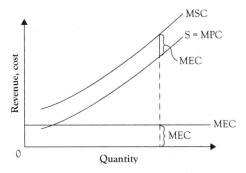

Figure 9-2. Marginal private cost, marginal external cost, and marginal social cost.

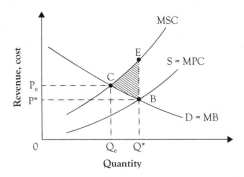

Figure 9-3. Resource misallocation with a negative externality.

to the production of this good. Note, too, that the price that is being charged, P*, is lower than the socially optimal price level (P_e) because the market has failed to account for all the costs of production.

The suboptimal output level imposes a deadweight loss of welfare on society. It is the area between the MSC curve and the marginal benefit curve over the range of "over-produced" units from Q_e to Q*—the triangle CEB.

Negative Externalities in Consumption

Negative externalities need not be present only when a good is being produced. They may arise when the good is being consumed—my use of my boombox in the local park may impose costs on those who have gone to the park for a quiet family picnic. In this case, the external cost is due to the use of the good, not its production. Similarly, tailpipe emissions from a car are a matter of externalities in consumption. The basic argument and the effects on optimal allocation of resources are identical, however, and Figure 9-3 can be reused.

The presence of negative externalities drives a wedge between the marginal private cost (which guides the decisions of producers) and the marginal social cost (which guides the optimal allocation of resources), causing an overproduction and underpricing of the good involved, and a deadweight welfare loss to society.

THINK IT THROUGH: Can you identify the negative externality in each of the following cases: second-hand smoking, traffic congestion during the evening rush hour, hog lagoons, wood stoves, pornographic magazines, and unsightly billboards? Is it an externality in production or in consumption?

Positive Externalities

Suppose you operate an apple orchard and your neighbor is a beekeeper. Her bees, in the act of producing honey, also provide pollination services for your apple trees—free. The activity of the beekeeper provides an external benefit for an individual who may not be directly involved in honey production, either as a producer or as a consumer. There can be positive externalities, either during the act of production of a good or service (as in this case) or in the act of consumption and, just as we saw with negative externalities, they cause a misallocation of resources.

Positive Externalities in Production

When a good such as honey is produced, that good bestows benefits on the purchaser and these benefits, internalized by the buyer, are reflected in the demand curve for honey. We can call these the *marginal private benefits* (MPB) of the good. These benefits are recognized in the marketplace and affect the profit-maximizing output level—the larger the benefit, the greater the demand and the higher the price of honey. The buyer

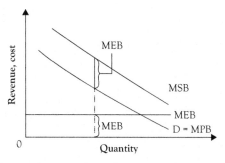

Figure 9-4. Marginal private benefit, marginal external benefit, and marginal social benefit.

may not be the only recipient of benefits—other members of society may also benefit from the production or consumption of the honey. In our example, the owner of the orchard receives additional benefits. We can call these benefits the *marginal external benefits* (MEB) of the good. For society, but not for the purchaser, the overall benefit of the good—its *marginal social benefit* (MSB)—is the sum of the private benefits and the external benefits. Owing to the presence of positive externalities, there is a difference between the benefits guiding market behavior and the benefits received by society.

This point is shown graphically in Figure 9-4. At each output level, the vertical distance between the MPB curve and the MSB curve is the extent of the marginal external benefits received by society during the production or consumption of the good.

If we now assume that there are no external costs, that is, that marginal private cost and marginal social cost are equal, we can incorporate the supply side into the analysis, as shown in Figure 9-5, and examine the consequences of the positive externality.

Market participants will establish the equilibrium price at P* and the equilibrium quantity at Q*, because that is where the demand and supply curves intersect. Society, however, would prefer a greater quantity to be produced, Q_e, albeit at a higher price, P_e, because this is where the marginal social benefit equals the marginal social cost. Because the private market has restricted output to Q*, there is a deadweight welfare loss to society represented by the triangle CEB.

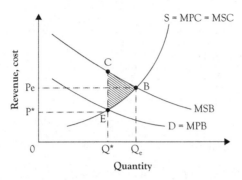

Figure 9-5. Resource misallocation with a positive externality.

Positive Externalities in Consumption

The analysis is entirely comparable if the positive externality springs from the act of consumption instead of production. Consider my recent purchase of the 5-CD boxed set retrospective on the storied career of the singer Neil Diamond. As a fellow fan of Neil, when you hear of my purchase of this difficult-to-find box, your first reaction may be to ask to borrow it for a few days. If I agree, then you are reaping a benefit from my purchase—the social benefit exceeds the benefit received by the purchaser. You may go further, burning illicit copies of your favorite tracks. As before, the presence of the externality leads to difference between the socially optimal level of sales of the good in question—Neil Diamond CDs—and the market provision.

Surely, this is the basis for the complaints by the music industry regarding all forms of file sharing and copies—that the market demand for music is less than it "should" be. With quantity at Q* and price at P*, clearly industry revenues are curtailed by the activity of file sharers.

THINK IT THROUGH: Can you identify the positive externality in each of the following cases: education, flu shots, a neighbor's beautifully kept garden, a neighbor who owns a pickup truck? Is it an externality in production or in consumption?

Internalizing Negative Externalities

Numerous measures have been proposed to correct for the resource misallocation caused by the presence of an externality. In some cases, more than one solution may be possible and which is the most effective solution will depend on the particular circumstances. Keep in mind that the goal is to influence the market to produce at the socially optimal output level.

Of the many options available to deal with a negative externality we consider five: private negotiation (the Coase Theorem), legal recourse, regulation, taxes, and a cap and trade system.

Private Negotiation

In 1960, Ronald Coase described how individuals should be able to negotiate a solution to alleviate the effects of an externality without government intervention. If the costs of negotiation are fairly low, then a socially optimal solution should be reachable.

Let us go back to the picnic in the park and my boombox. I enjoy my boombox, but, for others in the park, including you, the noise severely reduces their enjoyment of their picnic. We can still make a deal because I place some value of the music produced by my boombox whereas, for you and others, the boombox imposes costs—it's worth something to you to have me stop. Even if local noise ordinances are on my side, you and your fellow picnickers could still club together and bribe me to stop and, if local noise ordinances are in your favor then, if I value my boombox sufficiently highly, I could bribe you and your fellow picnickers to let me play it. Negotiation causes the costs and benefits *to society* to be internalized.

The *Coase Theorem* states that, even in the presence of externalities, an allocatively efficient solution can be achieved, as long as the transaction costs are low enough. Clearly, the smaller the number of individuals involved in the negotiation the easier it ought to be to reach an agreement. Let us examine the situation of Abercrombie and Fitch.

Suppose that Abercrombie runs a factory that pumps effluent into a river and that Fitch is a commercial fisherman who also uses the river. These are our two parties. Table 9-1 shows the profits earned each day by the two individuals.

If Abercrombie's factory pumps unfiltered effluent directly into the river, then Abercrombie's profit will be $230 and Fitch will net only $30 because many of the fish he hopes to catch will die. Without the filter, total profit for society is $260.

Table 9-1. Profit/Day for Abercrombie and Fitch

	Without Filter	With Filter	Gain/Loss With Filter
Abercrombie	$230	$200	–$30
Fitch	$30	$100	+$70
Total for Society	$260	$300	+$40

If Abercrombie's factory installs an effluent filter, then Abercrombie's profit will decrease to $200 but Fitch's profit will increase to $100. With the filter, the total profit for society is $300. From society's collective viewpoint, the filter should be used. However, let us suppose that no law exists that can force Abercrombie to use the filter—can the two parties negotiate an agreement that is mutually beneficial, as Coase predicts?

Clearly, following self-interest, Abercrombie should not install the filter. However, if Fitch pays (bribes) Abercrombie $40 per day to use the filter, then Abercrombie's profits would raise to $240, Fitch's profits would be $60 and both parties would gain. The lowest compensation that Abercrombie would accept is $30, whereas the highest compensation that Fitch would offer is $70—there is room for productive negotiation.

Now suppose the effects of pumping unfiltered effluent are as shown in Table 9-2. The profits when the filter is used are unchanged from the previous example. From society's collective viewpoint, the filter should not be used because the profit without the filter is $320 whereas the profit with the filter is only $300. Can the Coase Theorem prevail again?

In this case, even in the presence of environmental laws that could require Abercrombie to use the filter, a mutually beneficial agreement is possible. If, for example, Abercrombie offered Fitch $40 not to press forward with a law suit, then Fitch would gain, because the use of the filter would only increase his profit by $30. Abercrombie would also gain, as his profit of $210 is still higher than the profit he would earn if required to use the filter.

The important point to draw from these two cases is that, notwithstanding any law, if parties can easily negotiate, then a socially optimal outcome can be arrived at, just as Coase predicted. However, if there are many parties involved in the negotiation, or if negotiations are time-consuming, or if there are legal costs in establishing an agreement, then Coase's solution may become unworkable and another solution may be preferable.

Table 9-2. *Profit/Day for Abercrombie and Fitch*

	Without Filter	With Filter	Gain/Loss With Filter
Abercrombie	$250	$200	–$50
Fitch	$70	$100	+$30
Total for Society	$320	$300	–$20

Legal Recourse

If negotiation fails, then another option is to use the existing legal system, perhaps suing for damages, or requesting an injunction preventing the cause of an externality from continuing.

Regulation

In the absence of private negotiation, the government may intervene on behalf of society and impose environmental standards. In a case such as pollution from a smoke stack, the relevant may require the polluter to install filters or scrubbers, or some other form of treatment, to control the pollutants. The installation of antipollution gear has the effect of reducing the amount of pollution and also internalizing the cost of the pollution. Because the firm must now bear the cost of treating the pollution, its marginal private cost will increase, the effect being that the supply curve will shift to the left and output level will be reduced. Once again, the effect has been to internalize the externality to the responsible party.

THINK IT THROUGH: Cars produce emissions. To control the pollution, the government now requires that cars be fitted with expensive catalytic converters. Can you think of other examples of similar government intervention to correct spillovers?

Taxes

If it is impractical to require a firm to control its externality, then the government may impose taxes. Again thinking about pollution, an emissions tax is a tax levied on the quantity of pollution generated by a firm. Once more, the effect is to drive up the private cost for the firm (and the price for the users of the good). Output level will decrease. If the tax is levied appropriately, then the marginal private cost can be increased until it is equal to the marginal social cost and the allocatively efficient output level is achieved. The revenue received may be used by society to treat the pollution at the societal level or, perhaps, to compensate those who have been adversely affected by the pollution.

Cap and Trade Permits

The government may establish a maximum permissible amount of different kinds of pollutant. Consider sulfur dioxide. Let us say that a particular community's ecosystem can cope with 100 tons of sulfur dioxide emissions per time period—emissions beyond that amount will degrade the environment. The "cap" in this case is 100 tons of SO_2. The cap determines the supply of permits. If one permit grants the right to emit one ton of sulfur dioxide then only one hundred permits are available—the supply of permits is perfectly inelastic, as shown in Figure 9-6.

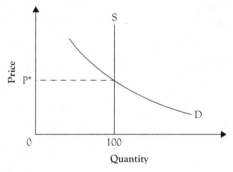

Figure 9-6. Pollution rights market.

The demand for permits depends on the desire of firms to pollute. Clearly, a market exists for pollution permits and an equilibrium price (P*) can be established. Firms now have an incentive to be more environmentally sensitive because, the greater the demand to pollute, the higher the price they pay. Firms pollute because the benefits to them exceed the costs so firms that garner smaller benefits from pollution will be unable or unwilling to buy pollution rights and will then cut production, move to another location, or (perhaps) go "underground." Firms that gain more from pollution will compete more aggressively for the right to pollute, resulting in pollution being caused by those who contribute the most valued output to society. A similar argument could be made with respect to carbon credits and, in fact, because of the need for an established market, carbon credits began to be traded formally in 2008.

THINK IT THROUGH: We can see some of these measures in the following example of disruptive dogs in a neighborhood. Suppose my dog barks, raids your trashcan, and digs up your garden. You may approach me and try to reach a solution. You may sue because of the noise and loss of amenity, or I may be required to build a fence to keep my dog inside my property (leash laws). Society may impose taxes on dog owners, or limit the number of dogs that a household may own. In its own way, each of these options is an attempt to correct for the overabundance of externality-causing dogs.

Internalizing Positive Externalities

There may be several alternative solutions for the misallocation of resources caused by the presence of positive externalities, with the most common being the provision of subsidies or regulation.

Subsidies

In the case of the beekeeper and the apple producer, where the bees are providing "free" pollination services for the orchard, there is an underallocation of resources to the production of bees and honey. For many years, the Agriculture Bill featured a "honey subsidy" designed to encourage additional honey production.

Regulation

Flu shots not only bestow benefits on the recipients, but they also bestow benefits on other members of the community because, with fewer persons suffering from influenza, the chances of contracting influenza are reduced. However, because flu shots involve some discomfort, inconvenience, and expense, a temptation exists to avoid having the flu shot—the demand for flu shots is lower than it should be. This tendency may be reduced if the cost of the shot is subsidized by the community but, even then, some individuals will balk. Aware of this tendency, many colleges require incoming students to have flu shots.

Public Goods

The second major market failure we consider in this chapter is that of public goods. Most goods are private goods. *Pure private goods* have two distinct characteristics—they are excludable and rivalrous—whereas *pure public goods* have neither of these characteristics. As we shall see, because public goods are nonexcludable and nonrivalrous, the free market will underallocate resources to their provision.

Excludability: Consider your car. Your car is a private good, owned by you. You may choose to share your car with others, but you do not have to. You can share the benefits of your purchase, but, if you wish, you can exclude them, retaining all of the benefits for yourself. One characteristic of your car, or of any private good, is that the benefits can be retained exclusively by the purchaser—there is a quality of excludability.

THINK IT THROUGH: As children, we are taught to share our crayons, our ball, and our toys, precisely because these are private goods!

Public goods do not possess the excludability characteristic—once they are purchased, it is not possible (or, at least, very difficult) to exclude others from the benefits of the good. Consider the classic example of a public good—a lighthouse. Once the lighthouse is in operation, its purchasers can receive the benefits, but so can everyone else! National defense is another example of a public good and the same issue arises—how can we prevent anyone from receiving the benefits of our defense system?

THINK IT THROUGH: Other examples of public goods include Fourth of July firework displays, our legal system, street lighting, public sanitation, broadcast TV and radio, and the fire service. Can you derive a (cheap) way of preventing any interested party from gaining the benefits of these goods?

Rivalry: Private goods are rivalrous meaning that you and I are in competition to receive such goods. Because this country has a very effective production and distribution system, we seldom notice this issue but when I buy a can of soup, or a Springsteen concert ticket, then that is one less available for you. We become aware of rivalry when there is a gas shortage, or there is a hurricane or other natural disaster that makes supplies short or demand unusually high.

THINK IT THROUGH: When the arrival of a hurricane or a severe snowstorm is imminent, we all dash off to buy milk, bread, beer, and batteries. Those who arrive at the convenience store a little too late find the shelves stripped bare by more alert rivals.

THINK IT THROUGH: Although broadcast TV and radio are nonexcludable and nonrivalrous, most such broadcasts are produced by private firms, because they have discovered that advertising can finance their activities. In fact, in the case of commercial TV and radio, the programming is no longer the good—the audience has become the good to be delivered to the sponsors.

Public goods, such as the lighthouse, are nonrivalrous. The beam from the lighthouse that provides safety for you also provides safety for me. The service I receive does not diminish the service you receive. Similarly, while our defense system is protecting me from incoming hostile missiles, it is providing you with no less protection than would otherwise be the case. Note that, if the good is nonrivalrous, then because additional recipients can be added without any need to increase the volume of the good or service, then the marginal cost of the good is zero!

THINK IT THROUGH: Confirm that mosquito control is a pure public good. Spraying to control mosquitoes provides benefits from which none can easily be excluded. Also, individuals are not in competition for the benefits.

Review: We have established two characteristics that distinguish private from public goods—excludability and rivalry. A pure private good has both characteristics; a pure public good has neither. Between these two extremes lie two other possible cases—club goods and common resources—as shown in Table 9-3.

A *club good* is excludable but nonrivalrous, an example being cable TV. Here, the service provided to me is not reduced if you become a subscriber (nonrivalrous) but, if you fail to pay your bill, your service can easily be terminated (excludable).

Table 9-3. Private Goods and Public Goods

	Rivalry	Nonrivalry
Excludability	Pure Private Good	Club Good
Nonexcludability	Common Resources	Pure Public Good

A *common resource* is rivalrous but nonexcludable, an example being clean water in a river. In this case, we are rivals—the more of the resource I use, then the less is available for your use—but it is fairly difficult for a private provider to exclude potential users or to charge for use of the resource.

THINK IT THROUGH: Which of the following are club goods and which are common resources—clean air, blue-fin tuna in the ocean, the post office, college lectures, computer software, wi-fi, national parks, digital music, public roads? The post office, college lectures, and computer software, wi-fi, and digital music are club goods; the others are common resources.

THINK IT THROUGH: If you travel to Britain and stroll around the older areas of some of the cities and keep your eyes open, then you still can see plaques on the walls of houses that were put there to identify the house as a client of a particular private fire service. The homeowner would pay the company to turn out to fight a fire at his home. In large towns, when an alert was sounded, two or more companies might arrive, but only one would fight *your* fire. Worse, if your company was occupied elsewhere, the other companies would stand by and let your house burn down, only springing into action when the fire spread to the house of one of their members! Clearly, this was a flawed system.

Tragedy of the commons: In the case of a common resource, because it is difficult to exclude users or to charge them for use of the resource, the tendency is for the resource to be overused. The resultant decline in the quality or quantity of the resource is known as the "tragedy of the commons." Common grazing land will be overgrazed; common fishing stocks will be overfished.

Considered purely from the viewpoint of individual self-interest, it makes sense to consume a good up to the point where one's marginal benefit is zero, because, by following that strategy, one's total benefit is maximized, at least in the current time period. Assuming that the marginal cost of the good is positive—if a meadow is grazed, then a cost is incurred—then this strategy will result in an overuse of the resource.

Dodos, the large flightless birds that lived on Mauritius in the Indian Ocean, provide a poignant example of the tragedy of the commons. Sailors, in need of fresh meat, found the birds easy prey and there was no authority preventing them from slaughtering the birds (nonexcludability) but the sailors were in competition because the more dodos were killed by one crew, the fewer dodos were left to breed and provide meat for future crews. Eventually, the dwindling numbers of surviving dodos became an eagerly sought "treat" and, accordingly, were slaughtered more enthusiastically when found. The dodo was extinct by 1662.

A similar fate befell the great auk. In this case, market forces played an even more significant role in the decline of the species because, with its increasing rarity, higher rewards were offered for skins or eggs. The last confirmed pair was slaughtered in 1844. The parallels with the poaching of ivory or rhino horns or the overfishing of tuna or cod should be clear— with dwindling stocks and rising rewards, the incentive to deplete further the resource becomes increasingly tempting.

The dodo and the great auk may not have died in vain because they left us with some insight into how to manage common resources more effectively. It is often said that "good fences make good neighbors." The British followed this advice in the 1700s, enclosing common grazing ground and granting private property rights to individuals. Better land management and increased agricultural productivity were the result. In general, if property rights can be assigned, better husbandry of resources is likely. In ocean fishing, harvest control rules, quotas, restrictions on the types of net used, and, in extreme cases, a suspension of fishing are all methods that have been employed to restrict excesses but in cases such as the oceans, the atmosphere, and the poaching of wide-ranging elephant or whale populations, property rights are often impractical to assign and the tragedy continues.

The Problem with the Private Provision of Public Goods

We have established that whereas some goods are pure private goods, others are pure public goods, and others, still, lie between the two extremes.

Let us restrict ourselves to pure public goods—those goods, such as a lighthouse, that are neither excludable nor rivalrous.

When we looked at common resources, we concluded that nonexcludability would cause consumers to wish to consume up to the point where marginal benefit is zero. That same condition is present for pure public goods. However, unlike common resources, pure public goods also have the characteristic of nonrivalry and, because of this, the marginal cost of providing additional service is also zero.

Herein lies the problem with the provision of pure public goods. Consumers will not wish to pay a price greater than the marginal benefit of the good (which is zero) and, with no possibility of excluding users, the supplier cannot charge a price higher than zero—no one will pay it. This is often referred to as the *free rider problem*. Further, the principle of efficient resource allocation we established in Chapter 6 was that marginal benefit (price) and marginal cost should be equal. With marginal cost at zero, there ought to be no price charged for the provision of the good. For a private firm, interested in earning profit, this situation is, of course, untenable and, therefore, left to its own devices, the private provision of public goods will either collapse entirely or, at best, be at an inefficiently low level.

Provision of public goods by society: Consider the following scenario. There is a small fishing community of ten families located in a bay on the North Carolina coast. Unfortunately, there are menacing rocks at the entrance to the bay and, every so often, a fishing boat is sunk and lives are lost.

The community does some research and discovers that the cost of installing and maintaining a beacon would be $3,600. It is estimated that the reduction in risk and the sense of security caused by the operation of the beacon is worth $1,000 to each family. A community meeting is called and it is proposed that each of the ten families should contribute $360. One ancient mariner—Salty Sam—objects, refuses to pay, and storms out. With nine families remaining, it is determined that each must make a contribution of $400 to fund the beacon. Unfortunately, another fisherman objects and leaves the meeting, leaving eight families each having to contribute $450 to finance the project. Note that, even at this point, a contribution of $450, in order to receive a benefit of $1,000 in peace of mind and reduced risk of shipwreck, is a good deal.

Nonetheless, it is probable that other families will refuse to pay—perhaps out of a sense of unfairness and being exploited by Sam and the other free riders—until, ultimately, either a less costly but less effective signal is set up or the beacon will not be built at all. A project that would yield a marginal benefit of $1,000 at a marginal cost of $360 may be abandoned.

Note, too, that the larger the number of individuals involved, the stronger is the incentive to refuse to volunteer funds—with millions of others contributing, who will miss the contribution of one individual?

In this situation, where voluntary contributions have failed to meet society's goal, the community may decide to provide the public good through compulsory contribution—taxes. Clearly, such compulsion is a long way from the voluntary self-interested interactions of the free market! Fortunately, most goods are private goods and consumers, by revealing their preferences and voting for the items they desire the most by purchasing them, signal to producers how society's scarce resources should be allocated.

Parting Thoughts

Welcome to the final section of the book. If you've read all nine chapters, then you've been challenged and worked hard, and you've encountered many economic concepts that I hope you will carry with you through life. Economics is the study of the choices we make as we pass through life—the world is our laboratory and our concepts are useless if we fail to apply them to that life. Certainly, you should have a sharper awareness of the transactions that surround you, the news that meets you each morning, and your perspectives on personal and global events.

At the very beginning of our first chapter, you were asked to imagine being in a restaurant and consulting the menu of choices. Economics is all about choice. We must make choices as we strive to achieve the best outcomes possible in our own self-interest. Individually and as a society we must make choices because, although we have unlimited wants, we have limited resources to meet those wants. Along the way, imperfections in the market mechanism or special considerations may make those choices difficult to realize, but the more aware we are of the imperfections and of the nature of the process itself, the more likely it is that our choices will serve us well.

My best wishes to you in the choices you make this day and in your future days.

Index

OTHER TITLES IN THE ECONOMICS COLLECTION

Philip Romero, The University of Oregon and Jeffrey A. Edwards,
North Carolina A&T State University, Collection Editors

- *Managerial Economics: Concepts and Principles* by Donald Stengel
- *Your Macroeconomic Edge: Investing Strategies for the Post-Recession World* by Philip J. Romero
- *Working with Economic Indicators: Interpretation and Sources* by Donald Stengel and Priscilla Chaffe-Stengel
- *Innovative Pricing Strategies to Increase Profits* by Daniel Marburger
- *Regression for Economics* by Shahdad Naghshpour
- *Statistics for Economics* by Shahdad Naghshpour
- *How Strong Is Your Firm's Competitive Advantage?* by Daniel Marburger
- *Game Theory: Anticipating Reactions for Winning Actions* by Mark Burkey

---

Announcing the Business Expert Press Digital Library

Concise E-books Business Students Need for Classroom and Research

This book can also be purchased in an e-book collection by your library as
- a one-time purchase,
- that is owned forever,
- allows for simultaneous readers,
- has no restrictions on printing, and
- can be downloaded as PDFs from within the library community.

Our digital library collections are a great solution to beat the rising cost of textbooks. e-books can be loaded into their course management systems or onto student's e-book readers.

The **Business Expert Press** digital libraries are very affordable, with no obligation to buy in future years. For more information, please visit **www.businessexpertpress.com/librarians**. To set up a trial in the United States, please contact **Adam Chesler** at *adam.chesler@businessexpertpress .com* for all other regions, contact **Nicole Lee** at *nicole.lee@igroupnet.com*.

CPSIA information can be obtained
at www.ICGtesting.com
Printed in the USA
FSOW03n1801300117
30213FS